Respecting Differences

Differences

A Guide to Getting Along in a Changing World

by Lynn Duvall

Edited by Pamela Espeland

Free Spirit
PUBLISHING

Library of Congress Cataloging-in-Publication Data

Duvall, Lynn, 1948–
    Respecting our differences : a guide to getting along in a changing world / by Lynn Duvall.
      p.   cm.
    Includes bibliographical references and index.
    ISBN 0-915793-72-5
    1. Respect for persons—Juvenile literature. 2. Prejudices—United States—Prevention—Juvenile literature. 3. Pluralism (Social sciences)—United States—Moral and ethical aspects—Juvenile literature. I. Title.
BJ1533.R42D88   1994
177—dc20   94-7164
                                                           CIP

Cover and book design by MacLean & Tuminelly
Index prepared by Eileen Quam and Theresa Wolner

10 9 8 7 6 5 4 3 2 1

Printed in the United States of America

The quotation from CBS Sunday Morning that appears on page 16 is © CBS Inc. 1993. All Rights Reserved. Originally broadcast on June 27, 1993 over the CBS Television Network. Reprinted by permission.

Free Spirit Publishing Inc.
400 First Avenue North, Suite 616
Minneapolis, MN 55401-1730
(612) 338-2068

Dedication

To Brooke, Kate, Mark, Jasen, Charles, and Davis,
who make me believe the future is in good hands.

Acknowledgments

Many thanks to Pamela Espeland, Judy Galbraith, and Liz Salzmann at Free Spirit Publishing for helping me turn my ideas into a book. Many thanks also to the staffs of *Teaching Tolerance* magazine and the *Klanwatch Intelligence Report*, and to Sallie Bodie, outreach coordinator for special projects at National Public Radio, for generously sharing information. Special appreciation to Sara Bullard, *Teaching Tolerance* editor, for putting me in touch with Free Spirit Publishing.

Contents

Introduction

"You don't have to love
everyone you meet,
but you don't have to
hate them either."

California eighth grader

1

A world of differences

By the time you finish school, the world will be a much different place than it is today. You know that technology is changing fast, and you recognize the need to learn computer skills so you can keep up. But the world is also changing *culturally*.

Already one in four Americans has African, Asian, Hispanic, or Native American ancestry. By the year 2050, that number will be one in three. More and more people of color—from South America, India, the Middle East, the Pacific Islands, and other places around the world—are making the United States their home. This increasing diversity is most obvious in the schools.

In a world with so many diverse groups of people, growing more diverse every day, human relations skills are just as important as computer skills. Probably more important.

Not many years from now, you'll be working with all kinds of men and women—young and old; conservative, moderate, and liberal; of various races, religions, ethnic backgrounds, and sexual orientations; and with different mental and physical abilities, problem-solving styles, and ways of responding to stress. Many of these people will have conflicting ideas about how and when it's appropriate for people to touch each other. They may disagree about when eye contact signals interest and assertiveness and when it's perceived as rude or threatening. Their privacy needs may vary depending on their ethnic heritage and family background, and they may not agree about how to behave in a work environment.

For example, let's say that a company hires a new employee who is Native American. One of his coworkers is a white American woman. The woman wants to make him feel welcome at his new job, so she asks him questions about his personal life—what neighborhood he lives in, where his wife works, how many children they have. To some white Americans, this is just being friendly. But to some Native Americans, it's an invasion of privacy. The man feels that the woman is nosy and impolite. She feels that he is aloof and unfriendly.

With so many confusing differences, how will we work together in the future? How can we work together today? How can we keep cultural differences from leading us to the wrong conclusions? How can we understand one another when we don't all speak the same language?

In the Oakland, California, city schools, the students speak *74 different languages.* Imagine being a teacher in Oakland! Unless you spoke 74 languages, you would have a hard time communicating with many of your students. How would you teach them geometry? Biology? How to use the library? How to find the bathroom?

When people are different—like the Native American and white American coworkers—misunderstandings happen. If they're not resolved, misunderstandings can create resentment, and resentment can lead to *stereotyping*—judging people without really knowing them. Stereotyping causes prejudice, irrational dislike, and suspicion. All of this can make it more difficult to attend school together, work together, and live together in communities.

That's why we need to learn to respect our differences. It's the only way we can get along in a changing world.

GOOD QUESTION

If four-fifths of the world's population consists of people of color, why are they still called "minorities"?

What's in it for you?

Respecting Our Differences can help you learn more about the people around you. The more you know about them, the harder it is to stereotype them and feel prejudice toward them. The less prejudice you feel, the less likely you are to treat other people unkindly or unfairly.

All of this goes both ways, of course. The more kindly and fairly you treat other people, the more likely they will treat you that way, the less prejudice they will feel toward you, and the harder it will be for them to stereotype you.

Getting along with all kinds of people takes *tolerance*—the capacity to recognize and respect the beliefs and practices of others, even when they are not exactly like you. This book can help you to become more tolerant of people who are (or seem) different from you.

If that sounds like a big job, remember that it's okay to start small. Everyone can learn to be more tolerant of *one* person or *one* group of people.

You may be thinking, "Why should I be more tolerant? What's in it for me?" Being more tolerant allows you to really get to know and enjoy the people around you and savor the rich variety of America's changing culture. The more tolerant you become, the more you'll get along with your classmates, coworkers, neighbors, and other people you see every day. You'll get better at communicating, thinking for yourself, understanding other people, and resolving conflict.

Conflict is a part of everyone's life regardless of gender, race, religion, or political beliefs. Unresolved conflict can lead to hurt feelings, resentment, even violence. It can keep you from doing and being your best at school, on the job, and other places and times in your life.

Respecting Our Differences can help you learn to "fight fair" by giving you ideas about how to deal with disagreements, power struggles, and feelings like frustration, resentment, and insecurity. These skills will make it easier for you to handle all kinds of uncomfortable situations. As a bonus, conflict resolution skills enable you to make better decisions and feel more confident about your ability to solve problems. You'll improve your relationships with your family and friends and have an easier time making new friends.

If you're not always comfortable with people who seem different from you, you're not alone. The students whose words you'll read throughout this book will encourage you to rethink your attitudes and see other people as worth appreciating, even celebrating. By listening to what they have to say, practicing empathy (putting yourself in someone else's place), and doing simple activities (called

"Time Outs") that have been designed to help you sort out complex issues and ideas, you'll start to recognize prejudices and where they come from. You'll start to unlearn your prejudices so you can get along better with everybody.

GOOD POINT

Just because you don't agree with somebody—or wouldn't do things the way he or she does—doesn't mean you can't respect each other and learn to get along.

Three reasons to become more tolerant

Have you ever heard someone say, "Give me one good reason why I should do that"? Here are *three* good reasons why you should become more tolerant.

1.   *The more you learn, the less you fear.* Remember when you were sure there were monsters under your bed? Or how afraid you were the first time you went swimming and put your face in the water? Then you looked under the bed and put your face in the water a few more times and suddenly you weren't afraid anymore. Unlearning prejudices works the same way.

Have you ever had a preconceived notion about a person, then found out you were wrong once you got to know him or her? That's how tolerance begins. Once you learn you have nothing to fear, you become willing to try more new things, ideas, and people. As you practice tolerance and become more comfortable with differences by experiencing them firsthand through relationships, curiosity replaces fear. Your mind opens. You start respecting other people's opinions, practices, and behaviors. You gain a deeper understanding of yourself and others.

It's easy to hate a stereotype, hard to hate someone you know and understand.

2.   *Tolerant people are more self-confident and comfortable in all kinds of situations.* Who wouldn't like to feel safer and more secure anytime, anywhere? Studies have shown that people who get along with different kinds of people are emotionally and physically healthier— and more successful in their careers—than those who don't.

3.   *Tolerance makes life more interesting.* What if you were allowed to read books by only one author? If you had to wear blue jeans, a white T-shirt, and black sneakers every day? What if you were never allowed to try anything new, not even a new soft drink or video game? What if all of your friends looked, thought, and behaved exactly alike? What if they all had to be the same age, religion, gender, and race?

Bo-ring.

That's what life without diversity would be like.

WE AREN'T ALL THE SAME

We aren't all the same beneath our different-colored skins. We aren't identical even without our different religions, genders, sexual orientations, and cultural backgrounds. But that doesn't mean we don't share important values, experiences, goals, and dreams. The key to getting along isn't to pretend that differences don't exist. Instead, we need to learn about differences, learn to accept them, and let ourselves enjoy them.

Any questions?

This book will help you answer some important questions. For instance:

- "What is prejudice and where does it come from?"

- "What are the good things about diversity? The hard things?"

- "Is it okay to tell sexist, racist, ethnic, AIDS, and other jokes if they're 'just jokes' and I'm 'only kidding'? What's the best response when I hear someone else tell a joke like that and it offends me or makes someone else uncomfortable?"

- "Why aren't there more people like me on TV or in newspapers and magazines?"

- "Why should I make friends with people who have different ideas and lifestyles?"

- "Why do some young people become skinheads?"

- "Should we set stricter limits on the number of immigrants coming to our country? Or should we admit anyone who wants to live here? If we do impose restrictions, how do we decide who to let in?"

As you read this book, you may come up with more questions of your own. Write them down. If you don't find the answers by the end of the book, you may want to do some additional research.

At the end of each chapter, you'll find a section called "Think About It, Talk About It" with even more questions for you to consider, share, and discuss with your friends and family.

Get in the habit of asking questions. This shows that you're willing to learn and grow, that your mind isn't made-up and closed.

Write to me!

If you *really* read this book, think about the questions, do the Time Outs, and learn from other people's experiences, you may find yourself changing in surprising ways. You may not be the same person when you finish reading as you are right now.

■ I want to know if and how this book affects your feelings, thoughts, opinions, and actions. Write to me and tell me.

■ I want to hear how diversity is making your life richer and more interesting. Drop me a postcard and let me know.

■ I want to read your stories about people you know, places you've been, and experiences you've had that relate to the issues covered in this book. Share your stories with me.

You can write to me at this address:

Lynn Duvall
c/o Free Spirit Publishing Inc.
400 First Avenue North, Suite 616
Minneapolis, MN 55401-1730

I hope to hear from you.

Lynn Duvall
Birmingham, Alabama

CHAPTER 1

It's Never Too Late to Change

"No matter how big or small, we all have a voice."

Student at a human relations workshop

Making a change

Twice a year, about 250 students and teachers crowd into a banquet hall at Birmingham–Southern College in Birmingham, Alabama, to participate in a program called "Make a Change." What do they hope to change using the ideas and skills they learn there? The world.

A big job, but somebody's got to do it. Or, as the students in the program might say, *everybody's* got to do it.

Listening to them talk, a visitor gets the impression that these young people have heard too many classmates called "fatso," "faggot," "Jew boy," "nigger," "retard," and other hurtful names—or have been called those names themselves. Maybe they've seen too many fights started by racist "jokes," heard about too many misunderstandings caused by ignorance, read about too much violence motivated by prejudice against people of a certain race, religion, gender, or sexual orientation. Many probably have personally felt the pain of being different—too dark-skinned or light-skinned, too smart or too dumb, too tall or too short, too fat or too thin. Maybe anything that sets them apart from their classmates can be and has been used against them.

As one female Asian American student later commented on a television special, "The ideal person in American culture is white and blonde—Barbie." These days, fewer and fewer people fit that description.

These students and teachers have come to "Make a Change" because they're ready to do something about intolerance, if only to look harder at their own prejudices.

EVERYBODY HAS PREJUDICES

Do you know anyone who thinks people of other races, religions, ethnic groups, and cultural groups aren't as smart, attractive, hardworking, or talented as people of their own group and, therefore, don't deserve the same rights?

Do you know anyone who feels uncomfortable around people who are different from them and, as a result, treats them differently, acts unfriendly toward them, avoids them, or even hates them and tries to hurt them?

Have you ever heard anyone say—in person, on television, or in a newspaper—that immigrants have no right to the same freedoms "real Americans" have struggled for? That homeless people could find work "if they really wanted to"? That women are "too emotional" to hold political office? That homosexuals shouldn't be allowed to teach school, join the military, or have children? That elderly people aren't good for much?

If you answered yes to any of these questions, then you have been exposed to racism, prejudice, and bias. If you have thought, said, or done any of these things yourself, then you have prejudices…just like everybody else.

If you've silently stood by while other people said or did any of these things, then you have condoned their actions. As one Wisconsin eleventh grader says, "If someone is referring to another racial or ethnic group in a negative way, tell them how you feel about it. Remaining silent only allows them to think that you believe the same."

The ups and downs of diversity

At first glance, the "Make a Change" group seems to reflect the popular racial stereotype of the Deep South—that everybody is either black or white. But first impressions are rarely as simple as they seem. That becomes clear when moderator Melissa Patrick, youth and education program specialist of the local chapter of the National Conference (founded as the National Conference of Christians and Jews), a group working to eliminate prejudice and discrimination, introduces a warm-up exercise called "Up/Down."

As she calls out some of the dozens of labels we use to categorize ourselves and others, people belonging to those groups stand up and are treated to loud, enthusiastic applause. Then they sit down until Melissa names another group. Quite a few people belong to so many groups that they don't spend much time sitting down .

The students and teachers applaud firstborn children, middle children, youngest children, only children, adopted children, twins, vegetarians, junk food "junkies," people with divorced parents, members of Adult Children of Alcoholics, Narcotics Anonymous, and other recovery groups, gay men and lesbians, kids with gay parents, kids with only one parent, people with a family history of mental illness, left-handed people, people with AIDS, and bilingual people. In short, they applaud many of the differences that make Americans unique—and the same characteristics that also can divide us, if we let them.

For some people in the program, "Up/Down" is the first time they have given positive feedback to people they don't feel comfortable with, don't understand, or normally dismiss as "not like me." It's the first time they have recognized that differences are normal and not necessarily bad, even if some of them don't quite believe it yet.

DEFINITIONS

Racism, prejudice, and bias are similar, but they are not the same.

- *Racism* is the belief that people of other races are inferior. This belief can lead to racist acts, which can take many forms: harassment (calling people names, painting racial slurs on their property, sending threatening notes), discrimination (withholding people's rights, not treating them as equals), even violence (assaults, bombings, and murders motivated by race).

- *Prejudice* is a feeling against (or for) something without any good reason. If you believe that a certain group of people is inferior because of their religion, gender, physical characteristics, race, or other characteristics, and you don't really know anything about the people themselves, then you are prejudiced against them.

- A *bias* is a preference that keeps you from making a fair judgment. A bias can be something as harmless as preferring strawberry ice cream over vanilla. Or it can be something potentially harmful, such as an employer preferring men over women, or a real estate agent preferring white people over people of color.

Beyond black and white

During the racial/ethnic heritage portion of "Up/Down," the initial black-and-white impression of the workshop participants expands to include Korean, Japanese, German, Asian Indian, and West Indian. There are students whose ancestry is Scandinavian, Italian, French, and British. Some claim several nationalities.

Religions included Catholic, Hindu, Quaker, Unitarian, Jehovah's Witness, and Baptist. There are atheists and agnostics in the group, too.

For just 250 people, the number of differences is surprising.

After "Up/Down" enlightens the students, teachers, and visitors about the infinite diversity of their small slice of humankind, some of the participants volunteer the reasons they came to the workshop and what they hope to gain from being there. Here are a few responses:

- "To stop racism and oppression."
- "To encourage communication."
- "To understand ourselves and the people around us."
- "No matter how big or small, we all have a voice."
- "To not feel alone."
- "To learn to change."
- "To meet people I wouldn't ordinarily meet."
- "To gain confidence and have a bigger voice in my school."
- "To open closed minds."

One young man wins the group's applause when he declares, "I'm here to associate, not to differentiate." He wants the group to know that he is making a conscious effort to mingle with all kinds of people instead of avoiding them because of their differences. He wants to be part of the crowd, not apart from it.

TIME OUT

Make a list of the groups you belong to. Be creative. See how many you can come up with.

For instance, I'm a right-handed, brown-haired, middle-aged, city-born, college-educated, white Southern writer, eldest child in a family of four girls raised by two rural-born alcoholic parents of Irish-English-French-Native American ancestry. My religious tendencies lean toward Zen Buddhism, and I'm a female.

That's part of the picture, anyway. What about you?

● ● ● ● ● ● ● ● ● ● ● ●

Getting personal with prejudice

Everybody has prejudices—you, me, your parents, teachers, neighbors, friends, acquaintances, relatives. Even great Americans and other famous people have prejudices. Some keep theirs hidden, but others let them show.

Inventor-statesman Benjamin Franklin once wrote: "German immigrants are clannish, ignorant and intent on maintaining their own language." Former President Dwight D. Eisenhower, who was widely considered the "typical American," was descended from those "clannish, ignorant immigrants" Franklin described.

Actor Mel Gibson, presidential candidate Pat Buchanan, Senator Jesse Helms, and former Los Angeles police officer Stacy Koon have all made sexist, racist, and/or homophobic remarks in interviews, speeches, and/or books. Marge Schott, owner of the Cincinnati Reds baseball team, found herself in the headlines when she referred to black team members as "million-dollar niggers" and made anti-Semitic remarks. (When it was learned that she owned a Nazi armband, she claimed it was part of a collection of World War II memorabilia.) Irish singer Sinead O'Connor shocked Catholics and non-Catholics alike by tearing a picture of Pope John Paul II in half on "Saturday Night Live." Rock and rap stars Guns 'N Roses, Public Enemy, Ice-T, and others have recorded songs with racist, sexist, and anti-Semitic lyrics.

Just because a remark is made by a public figure doesn't mean it's okay—or true.

Prejudice and the potential for change

Here are some facts about prejudice and stereotypes reported in National Public Radio's "Prejudice Puzzle" teacher's guide:

- By age three, children already exhibit prejudicial tendencies toward people based on physical characteristics. If these ideas are reinforced by people around them, they will develop into full-blown prejudices.

- From ages four to five, children stereotype gender behavior, express racial reasons for not playing with others, and show discomfort around disabled people.

- Between ages seven and nine, children develop what psychologists call "true racial attitudes," likely to be long-lasting.

- By age 12, children develop a complete set of stereotypes about all ethnic, racial, and religious groups.

The *Anti-Bias Curriculum* developed by the National Association for the Education of Young Children has this to say: "At two years old, children understand differences in race and gender. At two-and-a-half, they develop discomfort with differences. At three, they learn societal biases based on race and sex. At four, they start discriminating on their own."

But it's never too late to change. Just ask Anthony, an Italian American teenager who participates in a weekly race relations class at New Utrecht High School in Bensonhurst, New York.

In 1989, a mob of white teenagers in Bensonhurst murdered Yusef Hawkins, a black youth who was in the neighborhood to look at a used car. The white teenagers killed Hawkins because they thought he was going to a party being given by a white female teenager.

Attorneys Norman Seigel and Gaylen Kirkland decided that somebody needed to try to make peace between whites and blacks in Bensonhurst. So they started leading the once-a-week discussion at New Utrecht High. According to Anthony, it's working.

"It opened up my mind and made me realize that some of my opinions are unjust," he confessed on "CBS Sunday Morning." "To immediately dislike something because I don't know about it—that's not right. After a while, I learned to get along better with blacks, because I learned what their values are."

According to the National Conference, prejudice that comes from ignorance and stereotyping is the easiest to change. The best way to do that is with "purposeful interaction in schools and other educational settings"—in other words, by putting people of different races, religions, ethnic backgrounds, and sexual orientations to work together on different projects. In this book, you'll read about kids across the country who are doing just that.

SKJOLD PHOTOGRAPHS

SHADES OF RACISM

Racism isn't only between blacks and whites. It can involve people of any two or more races and even the same race. For instance, there is often tension between American blacks and Haitian blacks in Miami, and between Mexican nationals (Mexican citizens) and Mexican Americans in California. Asian Americans who have lived in the United States for years sometimes look down on new arrivals, who they call "F.O.B." ("Fresh Off the Boat").

Among people of color, there's often prejudice based on skin shade, with lighter skin being considered "better." Students at Hoffman Estates High School in Hoffman Estates, Illinois, explored this in a play called "Shades." The play was part of an Awareness-Raising Prejudice Reduction Campaign the students organized.

In one scene from "Shades," a group of young black women comment on seeing the same young black man with three young women, all with different skin colors.

At first they spot him with a light-skinned black woman:

First young woman (spitefully): "Well, here he comes with a red-bone on his arm. He just likes her because she's light-skinned."

Second young woman: "Black guys are always tryin' to get with the light-skinned as if we ain't good enough."

Group: "Girl, yeah!"

Later they see the young man with a dark-skinned black woman:

Second young woman: "What can he possibly see in her? I don't understand how a brother could like her, she's so dark and crusty. She's so black she's blue."

Later the young man comes walking by with a white woman, and the three make more disparaging comments. Then, when he walks by alone:

Third young woman: "He must be gay!"

Finally the young man has a chance to speak:

Young man: "I don't understand. When I was with a light-skinned girl, I was wrong. When I was with a dark-skinned girl, I was wrong. But am I really the one who is wrong? I don't know. All I know now is that I am alone."

Adapted from "Shades," written by and starring Heather Nelson, Latasha Moree, Andre Fountain, Nashunda Stevens, Sandy Sanders, Margaux Sinclair, Karien Wooldridge, Kevilee Potts, and Khaleelah Jones, 1992. Used with permission.

1.   Think of your best friend. How many different groups does he or she belong to? Make a list, then check it with your friend. How close is your list to the truth? Is it too long? Too short? What important groups did you miss when describing your friend? Did you make any wrong or inaccurate assumptions?

2.   Imagine that you're part of the "Make a Change" program. What is your reason for coming to the workshop?

3.   What are some of your prejudices? Where do they come from? Are you comfortable with your prejudices? Why or why not?

4.   Has there ever been a time when you were completely wrong about another person because of a prejudice?

5.   Read a recent newspaper and look at ads, or listen to a popular music recording or watch the video. Can you find or do you hear any prejudicial remarks?

6.   Have you ever worked together with people of different races, religions, ethnic backgrounds, and/or sexual orientations?

7.   Do you remember when you first noticed differences between races?

Getting along in a changing world...

Hoffman Estates High School: Where "People Are People"

"People Are Different. Expect It. Respect It."
From the "People Are People" program

Not everybody at Hoffman Estates High School in Illinois thought Black History Week and Women's History Week were good ideas. Some students made racist and sexist remarks about them. Others wondered "Why don't we have a White History Week? A Men's History Week? Why do blacks and women deserve special treatment?" Still others just refused to participate.

These responses disturbed some students at the school, so they decided to take action, to work to encourage tolerance and understanding. At first, only seven people showed up at the brainstorming sessions they held. But word got around, and soon more than 50 people gathered to offer ideas and energy.

The first year, the group—which eventually would be called the Cultural Awareness Club—produced an ambitious Awareness-Raising Prejudice Reduction Campaign with a special event called "People Are People." The front of the program proclaimed, "People Are Different. Expect It. Respect It." The event included student-produced videos and plays dealing with all kinds of prejudice. Dark-skinned blacks insulted light-skinned blacks. Puerto Ricans stereotyped whites. In one skit, a Joker told "funny" stories about Hispanics, Indians, women, and Jews.

"People Are People" got students thinking, talking, and interested in organizing other events. They produced a video dealing with diversity-related issues titled "Just Ask." Then came a weeklong Cultural Diversity Celebration, a Youth Leadership Seminar, and a series of panel discussions where participants set goals and later published them in a newsletter. The main goal: To create an environment of mutual respect.

They're still working on that goal, and they know it won't be easy. As the "People Are People" statement says: "Our purpose is not to attempt to abolish prejudice and tell all of you to love one another. It is simply an attempt to lessen the great fears we all have and replace them with an acceptance of difference."

The students at Hoffman Estates High School would probably be the first to admit that they have a long way to go. But look how far they've come…from a meeting with just seven people.

Compiled with information from "HumaNews," a Human Relations, Inc., newsletter, June 1993; "People Are People: An Awareness-Raising Prejudice Reduction Campaign," 1992; and information provided by Denise Mack, social science teacher and "People Are People" co-sponsor, 1992–1993.

CHAPTER 2

Starting Small

"Just saying 'hi' can't be too hard."

Connecticut tenth grader

Learning about diversity

Fifteen students sit in a circle at the Jewish Community Center in Birmingham, Alabama. They come from different schools, different neighborhoods, different racial, ethnic, and religious backgrounds, different kinds of families. Some are talkative and enthusiastic. Others seem shy and self-conscious when it's their turn to talk. At least one seems cynical beyond her 17 years.

But they all have something in common that transcends their superficial dissimilarities: They believe they can help improve human relations in their schools and communities. And they're willing to do their share of the hard work needed to make that happen.

That's why they get together one Sunday afternoon each month to share their frustrations, fears, hopes, and ideas, and to talk about how cultural diversity affects their relationships and their schools.

These students are typical of young people around the world who are challenging prejudice and learning to accept—even celebrate—racial and cultural diversity. They're learning to speak up about the injustice and discrimination they encounter when someone tells a sexist joke, makes fun of overweight or elderly teachers, deliberately excludes a classmate with a disability, or diminishes or disrespects someone in another way.

They start within the safety of their monthly group, exploring their feelings, brainstorming solutions to problems, role-playing with other group members. Before long, they become confident enough to confront real conflict and speak up for themselves and their classmates.

They're also learning to appreciate the fact that America's diversity gives us one of the richest cultures on earth. We don't have to travel to other countries to enjoy the food, language, music, art, literature, religious rituals, and celebrations of dozens of different groups. Just walking down the street can be a multicultural experience these days.

"I think that people should get to know each other," an East Hartford, Connecticut, tenth grader told *Teaching Tolerance* magazine. "In my high school, I think I'm very fortunate. We have every race, religion, ethnic group, everything. I think that people should not be afraid; just saying 'hi' can't be too hard. My generation and the way we feel are going to be the future, and if people want to stop racial and ethnic conflicts it has to start now with us."

Even in average-size cities, residents often have access to Australian, Spanish, and Italian movies, Indonesian gamelan (stringed instruments) orchestras, Mexican craft demonstrations, Haitian art exhibits, and performances by Chinese and Laotian dance troupes, as well as a mind-boggling variety of foods— Ethiopian, Mesopotamian, Cuban, Korean, South American, Cajun, Creole, Malaysian.

Enjoying the treasures of other cultures gives us new ways of appreciating our own. Even a simple activity like trying a new dish can arouse our curiosity about other ways of life and whet our appetites for other new ideas and experiences.

If you've eaten Mexican, Italian, Chinese, Cajun, and American food, you may think you've tasted all the flavors there could possibly be. You haven't. Try some complex, aromatic Thai food. Or some tart, earthy Persian dishes. Or a crumbly French pastry dipped in chocolate. Or the new ethnic restaurant that just opened in your neighborhood.

TIME OUT

In Chapter 1, you made a list of the different groups you belong to. Now try to come up with a list of things you have in common with people from other groups. Make this list as long as your first one…longer, if you can.

Next, make a list of foods, films, books, or music relating to other cultures that you tried this year. Make a list of things you'd like to try in the coming year.

● ● ● ● ● ● ● ● ● ● ●

Changing the world one person at a time

Someone once said, "The only constant is change." That realization drives some young people to learn as much as they can about the changes around them and the changes to come.

Damon, Tim, Amanda, Elaina, and the other students at the Jewish Community Center spend their hour discussing the tension, disagreements, and resentments that develop between racial and cultural groups. They brainstorm possible solutions using conflict resolution techniques and communication skills they learned at "Anytown USA," a National Conference summer camp designed to help students recognize and overcome prejudice and discrimination.

Back at their schools, armed with new skills, understanding, and motivation, the "Anytown" graduates go to work. They organize multicultural awareness programs, field trips to Civil Rights museums and memorials, graffiti paint-overs, and community service projects that bring together teenagers and senior citizens from varied cultural backgrounds. "Anytown" graduates from Rachel's school formed the Forum for Cultural Diversity and participated in service projects such as an AIDS fundraising walk and low-income house-building. They also asked for information about Black History Month to be integrated into the curriculum at their predominantly white school, as well as information about how various ethnic groups celebrate Christmas.

Tina and some of her classmates volunteer for a program run by a local community school. The purpose of the program is to bridge the gap between teenagers and senior citizens. Tina also volunteers at the Jimmie Hale Mission, a shelter for homeless men, where she helps serve dinner and talks to men she might otherwise never get to know.

In Pennsylvania, students involved in the Philadelphia Young Playwrights Festival use drama to explore and create empathy about similar issues. Their plays have dealt with topics including a young man who is learning to accept his brother's homosexuality, three students who discover that they all have disabled siblings, a young African American who is trying to understand her place in black history, and a young woman who discovers that a young man she's attracted to has AIDS.

These students and thousands of others believe that their efforts, no matter how small they may seem, can add up to big change, enhancing unity and understanding in their schools and the diverse communities they serve. And, since the world is an enormous collection of communities, they hope their actions will change the world slowly, surely, one person, one project at a time.

BLAZING A NATIONAL HISTORIC TRAIL

Students all over the country are working to help make the route of the Selma to Montgomery voting rights marches of 1965 a National Historic Trail. The marches, led by Dr. Martin Luther King, Jr., resulted in passage of the Voting Rights Act, which guaranteed black citizens the right to vote for the first time in their 300-year history in the United States.

The students who wanted the march route designated a National Historic Trail sent memos to the National Park Service. The memos, titled "Reasons to remember the Selma to Montgomery March and ways the march can be commemorated," will be included in a report to Congress.

Here's one reason from Staten Island tenth grader Toniesha Morton that was reprinted in *Teaching Tolerance* magazine: "It is important to remember the Selma to Montgomery march because...all races banded together for the beliefs that the U.S. was built on. This march like others was not only for blacks; it was for humanity."

For more information about the trail, write to:

Selma to Montgomery Trail Study
National Park Service
75 Spring Street S.W.
Atlanta, GA 30303

A force for positive change

It may seem hard to believe that small groups of committed individuals can change the world, but as anthropologist Margaret Mead once observed, "It's the only thing that ever has." When thousands of small groups work toward the same goal, they become a massive force for positive change. You may think, "I'm just a kid. What can I do?" But even one person can make a difference.

Children played a vital role in the Civil Rights Movement—children like Sheyann Webb of Selma, Alabama. During the 1960s, when Sheyann was eight years old, she and her friend Rachel began attending voting rights mass meetings, where they learned and led freedom songs and heard speeches about discrimination against black voters.

Even though blacks had been given the right to vote in 1870, many officials made the voting registration tests so difficult that no one could pass them. Whites didn't have to take the tests. This meant that blacks technically had the right to vote, but not in reality.

Not until the Voting Rights Act was passed in 1965 were blacks *guaranteed* the right to vote. That means that during your parents' lifetime, even though a large percentage of the U.S. population was black, these men and women had little or no voice in selecting the officials who made important decisions about their lives. Sheyann, Rachel, and the other children who marched in protests led by Dr. Martin Luther King, Jr.—a champion of civil rights for all races—helped to change that.

Young people are still making a difference. In 1991, 12-year-old Ashley turned her outrage against Nazi video games into a law prohibiting their import into the United States. In the games, players earn points for killing Jews. Ashley started a petition against the games and collected hundreds of signatures. Eventually she recruited lawmakers to lobby against the games on her behalf, and the law was passed.

Ashley first heard about the games when she was watching a news broadcast with a segment about Nazi video games popular in Austria, Germany, and underground in the U.S. She felt that the games promoted genocide and were a bad influence on the children playing them, and she decided to try to do something about them. For her efforts and commitment, Ashley won the 1991 Youth in Action Human Rights Award from the Anti-Defamation League of B'nai B'rith.

People United for a Better Oakland, a community improvement group, had been more-or-less abandoned due to lack of interest when Angela came along in 1991. The concerned teenager reorganized the group. She believed that a textbook being offered to local schools was racist and biased, and she needed community support to take a stand. She went to school board meetings and talked to a lot of people, and the textbooks were rejected. But she later found out that some schools were using them anyway, so she's still working on it.

SYMBOLS OF PEACE

According to *Teaching Tolerance* magazine, a group of students at an Albuquerque, New Mexico, elementary school decided to start a peace movement to honor young victims of war. Their goal: a children's peace statue. Along with children from 17 other New Mexico schools, they formed the Kids Committee for Children's Peace Statue and published a newsletter about their plans to dedicate the statue in 1995.

They were soon joined by students from 49 states and 45 countries, who together contributed $10,000. Children everywhere are invited to send additional donations as well as peace poems and songs, names of children who support world peace, and "peace cranes," pieces of paper folded to form cranes, a Japanese symbol of peace. Children send thousands of peace cranes every year to Hiroshima, the site of the first atomic bomb dropped on a city, where almost 130,000 people died in 1945.

In Redwood Falls, Minnesota, children folded 1,000 cranes for a children's hospital and a retirement home. At a 1991 peace ceremony, they presented 1,000 more cranes to local families with a loved one in the Persian Gulf.

To find out more about the Children's Peace Statue, send a stamped, self-addressed, legal-size envelope to:

>Kids Committee
>P.O. Box 12888
>Albuquerque, NM 87195-2888

For information about the paper crane club, write to:

>Charles Numerick
>1000 Crane Club
>1126 Gibbs Avenue
>St. Paul, MN 55108

"I'm just a kid. What can I do?"

Your contribution doesn't have to be as newsworthy as Sheyan's, Ashley's, or Angela's to make a difference. You don't have to write to the National Park Service or plan a statue. You don't even have to fold paper cranes. You can make a difference simply by encouraging the people around you to look at each person as an individual and treat him or her with respect. You can behave that way yourself, as an example to others.

SKJOLD PHOTOGRAPHS

SKJOLD PHOTOGRAPHS

SKJOLD PHOTOGRAPHS

Sometimes it's enough to be kind to just one person, maybe someone all the other kids usually ignore or tease. When Pamela was 13, the popular girls in her school made fun of a classmate named Nancy who was mentally disabled. One day Pamela walked into the girls' restroom and found a group of them putting makeup on Nancy—makeup that made her look like a clown. They were telling Nancy how beautiful she was, and Nancy was oblivious to their cruelty.

"At that point in my life," Pamela remembers, "I was just figuring out what kind of behavior was tolerable to me and what was not. I didn't say anything at the time because I was kind of a nerd myself, and I couldn't afford to attract the attention of the popular girls. But I paid a lot more attention to Nancy after that. I always said hello when I saw her in the halls. That's what I did in my own little way, and it has reflected throughout my life. Now, if there's someone that everyone else is treating badly, I figure it's up to me to be kind."

TIME OUT

Being scared and feeling some pain and anger can be useful. Try to remember a time when you felt afraid, hurt, and angry because of someone else's words or actions. Focus on those feelings. Let yourself experience them again. The next time you see someone being discriminated against, recall your painful feelings and do something about the injustice you see.

In his book, *A Gathering of Heroes: Reflections on Rage and Responsibility,* African American writer Gregory Alan-Williams describes how his own memories of being taunted and threatened inspired him to rescue a Japanese American man who was being beaten by a group of black youths during the 1992 Los Angeles riots. Remembering his feelings motivated him to take action.

This suggestion comes from the National Conference "Anytown USA" workshop. For more information about this summer camp and other National Conference programs, write or call:

> The National Conference
> 71 Fifth Avenue
> Suite 1100
> New York, NY 10003
> Telephone: (212) 206-0006

● ● ● ● ● ● ● ● ● ● ●

Starting small

Take your cue from the motto of the Esprit clothing company: "Be informed. Get involved. Make a difference." Choose one social problem to familiarize yourself with and commit to; that way you won't get overwhelmed and give up. You don't have to start or lead a crusade. Just learn enough to educate and motivate others so they can get involved and make a difference, too.

Cynthia Moran, 15, from South Berwick, Maine, and Toby Gillen, 16, from Tulsa, Oklahoma, work with senior citizens. Toby says, "Some kids think the elderly are really different—but I think they still have the same hopes and dreams as kids. They are really fun and always carry smiles on their faces."

"I have two friends who are senior citizens," adds Cynthia. "They love me so much, and I love them back. One of them said to me recently, 'Nobody has loved me like this before.' Some people don't want to be friends with old people because they're afraid the old people are going to die, but you should know that even if they do die, you made a difference in their lives."

READ MORE ABOUT IT

Toby Gillen and Cynthia Moran are highlighted in a book called *150 Ways Teens Can Make a Difference: A Handbook for Action* by Marian Salzman and Teresa Reisgies with thousands of teenage contributors (Princeton, NJ: Peterson's Guides, 1991). If you want to meet more young people like them, you might want to read this book.

Free Spirit Publishing, the publisher of the book you're reading now, has several titles that feature young people who are working for change. You might want to read these books, too:

■ *The Kid's Guide to Social Action: How to Solve the Social Problems You Choose—and Turn Creative Thinking into Positive Action* by Barbara A. Lewis (Free Spirit Publishing, 1991)

- *Kidstories: Biographies of 20 Young People You'd Like to Know* by Jim Delisle (Free Spirit Publishing, 1991)
- *Kids with Courage: True Stories about Young People Making a Difference* by Barbara A. Lewis (Free Spirit Publishing, 1992)
- *Girls and Young Women Leading the Way: 20 True Stories about Leadership* by Frances A. Karnes and Suzanne M. Bean (Free Spirit Publishing, 1993)

1.   What is your school doing to increase your understanding of racial and cultural diversity? What could you do to help?

2.   Have you ever seen classmates making fun of a student who was "different" from them in some way? What did you do? If you ignored the incident, imagine how the student felt. Then imagine how he or she would have felt if a classmate had stepped in and taken his or her side.

3.   What issues do you feel most strongly about? Racism? Sexism? Homelessness? What are some small steps you could take toward being a positive force for change?

Getting along in a changing world...

Mediation:
Kids Helping Kids Resolve Conflict

"The Vietnamese are our brothers,
the Russians are our brothers,
the Chinese are our brothers:
and one day we've got to sit down
together at the table of brotherhood."

Dr. Martin Luther King, Jr.

Maybe you're used to teachers or other adults settling disputes between classmates. But today in many schools across the country, conflict resolution means students helping students solve problems. When two students have an argument, a fight, or a misunderstanding, a third student trained as a mediator—someone who helps to settle differences—steps in and guides them to a peaceful solution.

After hours of study and practice, student mediators learn how to listen without interfering or blaming, how to remain calm when tempers flare, and how to help the people involved in disputes communicate their feelings without making things worse.

SKJOLD PHOTOGRAPHS

At a school in the Bronx, a cultural misunderstanding—a difference in the way two cultures interpret behaviors—led to a conflict between some Southeast Asian students and a group of black and Latino kids. When a Cambodian and a black student bumped into each other, the black student tried to speak to the Cambodian student, who refused to look at him. The more the black student tried to talk to the Cambodian, the more the Cambodian turned away. The incident ended with a chase and a fight.

During mediation, the black student explained that he felt the Cambodian was being disrespectful by not making eye contact. The Cambodian explained that he had been confused, and that he was trying to prevent a fight by not looking at the black student.

Here are some of the guidelines the mediator used in helping to resolve this dispute. You might try them yourself the next time you have a problem with a classmate, family member, or friend:

1.   State your feelings clearly, without accusing the other person. Begin with "I feel…" instead of "You always…." For instance, instead of saying, "You always look away when I try to talk to you," the black student could say, "I feel like you don't want to talk to me when you look away." That way, he's talking about how he feels, not judging the other person.

2. Never interrupt or finish another person's sentences.

3. Concentrate on what is being said, not on what you're going to say when the other person is finished talking.

4. Maintain eye contact with the other person.

5. Ask questions to make sure you understand what the other person means.

6. To let the other person know that you're listening and you understand his or her side of the story, repeat what you think the other person is saying.

7. Never put down the other person.

Adapted from "The Peacekeepers: Students use mediation skills to resolve disputes" by Michael Meek, *Teaching Tolerance*, Fall 1992, pp. 46-52.

RULES FOR FIGHTING FAIR

Fighting Fair: Dr. Martin Luther King, Jr., for Kids includes six "Rules for Fighting Fair" that can help you know what to do in conflict situations. Try them and see if they work for you.

1. Identify the problem.

2. Focus on the problem.

3. Attack the problem, not the person.

4. Listen with an open mind.

5. Treat a person's feelings with respect.

6. Take responsibility for your actions.

Written by Fran Schmidt and Alice Friedman. The Grace Contrino Abrams Peace Educational Foundation, Inc. 1990. All Rights Reserved. Reprinted by Permission.

CHAPTER 3

Unlearning Our Prejudices

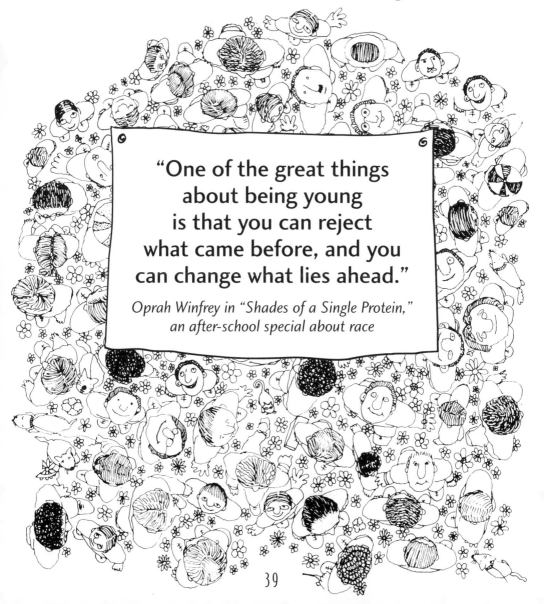

"One of the great things
about being young
is that you can reject
what came before, and you
can change what lies ahead."

Oprah Winfrey in "Shades of a Single Protein,"
an after-school special about race

What's the difference?

Differences are always disturbing. No matter how fair-minded we think we are, we feel most comfortable when we can establish common ground with other people. But today the world is changing so much so quickly that we may have to look a little harder for similarities.

Emily, a student from Ashland, Oregon, told *Teaching Tolerance* magazine, "I feel uncomfortable around people of different races…because I'm not used to them, and I'm afraid I'll offend them."

How do you feel around Asian Americans, African Americans, European Americans, skinheads, Muslims, people with epilepsy or Down Syndrome, heterosexuals, homosexuals, environmentalists, Rastafarians, and Cajuns? If you don't spend much time with people from those groups, what do you imagine they're like? Why? Where did you get your ideas?

Being uncomfortable with differences is human nature. So is having prejudices. The trouble is, prejudices can lead to discrimination, unfair treatment, and illegal acts like denying someone a job, housing, a raise, or a promotion because of race, religion, gender, national origin, or sexual orientation. Prejudice can even lead to violence—cross burnings, firebombings, gay bashings, murders.

Some scholars say that the first written account of racial discrimination appeared in the 14th century, more than 600 years ago. So prejudice is nothing new, but that doesn't mean history has to keep repeating itself.

After all, you weren't born with prejudices. Just as you learned to walk, talk, and think, you learned prejudices from your family, friends, teachers, and neighbors. You learned them from newspapers, movies, TV, and books. Because you learned them, you can also *unlearn* them. You can decide to think for yourself, to gather new information, to ask questions and keep an open mind.

You can also develop prejudices through bad experiences with people. Over the past five years, 14-year-old Amy's father was robbed three times by groups of young black men. As a result, he's suspicious of all groups of young black men. Do you think it's possible that you might react in the same way?

TIME OUT

Think of three common stereotypes you believe or prejudices you have. If you can't think of any right away, try a technique called "free association":

1.   Across the top of a sheet of paper, write the names of three different groups. (For instance, "Texans," "Football players," and "Skinheads.")

2.   Add "all" or "always" to each name. (Examples: "Texans all/always," "Football players all/always").

3.   Underneath each name, write the first three things that come to mind. Don't stop to think. Just write.

Your examples might look something like this:

- "Texans all own oil wells and wear boots and cowboy hats."

- "Football players all get lousy grades, take steroids, and date the best-looking girls."

- "Skinheads all hate blacks, Jews, and gays and beat people up all the time."

Where do you think you learned your stereotypes? Do you have class-mates, relatives, or friends who feel the same way? How about TV, movies, the newspaper? (By the way, how many Texans, football players, and skinheads do you know personally?)

● ● ● ● ● ● ● ● ● ● ● ●

Where are the people like us?

Lots of people get their ideas about dwarves, or little people, from *The Wizard of Oz* and other fantasy films. Do you have any stereotypes about dwarves? Such as "maybe they're cute, but they can't really do anything"? Or "they belong in fairy tales, not in real life"? Or "they should join the circus"?

If Jason, an African American dwarf in Beaufort, South Carolina, had listened to the stereotypes, he might be sitting at home feeling sorry for himself. But because he had parents who encouraged him to do and be his best, Jason is living a full and active life. He belongs to ROTC and works in a supermarket after school. He has won trophies in karate, is a good wrestler, and enjoys break dancing. Most of his classmates like him and enjoy his sense of humor. Other people admire him, too. Jason was even featured in a National Public Radio special project series, "The Prejudice Puzzle."

"It amazes me sometimes the things I've been able to do," Jason says, "because people have said I'd never be able to lift weights, run track, play any sports. People said 'just do good in school, get an A average, and become a doctor or something… because you're just too little to do anything else.'"

Dwarves aren't the only people who are frequently stereotyped in films. The popular movie *The Prince of Tides* was sensitive to many important issues—aging, family conflict, the emotional cost of keeping painful secrets. But it portrayed a main character's gay next-door neighbor as effeminate, self-mocking, and campy. This stereotype has been around as long as gay characters have been featured in mainstream movies, which hasn't been all that long. It's a handy, "no-brainer" characterization, easy for writers to write, easy for actors to portray, and easy for much of the heterosexual public to accept. This movie, which was inspired by a best-selling novel, turned another major character into a minor one, never mentioning that she was a lesbian.

Movies today are full of the same stereotypes your parents and their parents grew up with: the dumb blonde; the surfer dude; the tough guy with a heart of gold; the "easy" (sexually active) woman who "gets what she deserves" (a knife in the heart or an ax in the head); the poor girl who makes good by being honest and working hard; the ambitious businessman who sacrifices everything for his job, only to find that his life away from work is empty and meaningless. Today they're just wearing different clothes, using different slang, drinking sparkling water and espresso instead of martinis or tequila, and listening to reggae instead of big band music or jazz.

How many of these familiar stereotypes have you seen in movies?

- The Arab—wealthy businessman, religious zealot, violent terrorist
- The Latino or Chicano—maid, gardener, gang member
- The Asian American man—Kung Fu master, gardener, gang member
- The Asian American woman—dainty, submissive "butterfly" or evil "Dragon Lady"
- The African American—maid, butler, gardener, gang member, drug dealer
- The Native American—bloodthirsty, ignorant, dirty savage, half-breed, noble savage.

Then there are some stereotypes you probably haven't thought much about. For instance, when the Walt Disney film *Hocus Pocus* opened in the theaters, a group of witches called a press conference to object to the negative stereotype portrayed in the movie. The three main characters were scatterbrained and clumsy and constantly making trouble with their wicked spells. Real witches, said the protesters, are intelligent, organized, and devoted to doing good.

The entertainment industry argues that they're presenting the images the public wants to see. Do you agree? Why do you think we don't see more varied and complex characters more often in a wider variety of social and professional roles?

Where are the people like you, like me…like us? When was the last time you saw a movie or TV character you could really identify with? Or one who reminded you of your mother, your teacher, your uncle, your neighbor, your best friend?

SKJOLD PHOTOGRAPHS

If this bothers you, speak out. Write to the movie companies and the TV networks. Tell them you're tired of seeing stereotypes and you'd like to see some real people in their movies and programs for a change. You might ask your classmates, friends, and family to sign the letter, too. The more signatures, the better. You can find addresses and names of people to write to by contacting your local TV stations. Or go to the library and look for *The Address Book: How to Reach Anyone Who's Anyone* by Michael Levine (New York: Putnam, 1993).

If you don't think you can make a difference, remember Ashley and Angela from Chapter 2.

TIME OUT

Can you think of three current movies that feature any of the stereotypes described on page 43? Keep a list of the stereotypes you spot in the movies, on TV, and in magazines for the next month or two. You may be surprised at how common these stereotypes are.

● ● ● ● ● ● ● ● ● ● ●

Stereotypes in the news

Stereotypes in movies and on TV may not surprise you anymore, but even "educational" activities like reading the newspaper or watching TV news broadcasts can perpetuate stereotypes and encourage prejudices.

The Navajo word for reporter translates as "gossip teller." Because the Navajo believe that journalists meddle in private affairs and misrepresent the truth, journalists often are not allowed on Navajo pueblos. And there are other reasons. In 1993, many Navajo people became ill and some even died from a strange new virus. The media referred to it as "the Navajo flu." How would you like to have a lethal virus named after your ethnic group?

Broadcast and print media stories also may support stereotypes by presenting only one view of a controversial issue. For instance, features on "welfare mothers," immigration quotas, and hate crimes may not tell the whole story.

LOADED WORDS

Many minority groups share the view that the media perpetuate stereotypes about them. An Asian Pacific American group addressed the problem in *Asian Pacific Americans: A Handbook on How to Portray Our Nation's Fastest Growing Minority Group,* published in 1989 by the National Conference of Christians and Jews, the Asian American Journalists Association, and the Association of Asian Pacific American Artists. According to that publication, certain stereotypes have become associated with certain groups, and "loaded words" are often used to describe individuals who belong to those groups. This reinforces stereotypes and prevents readers and viewers from appreciating people as unique individuals.

Here are examples of "loaded words" that are often used by the media to describe Asian Pacifics:

- Serene, shy, quiet, reserved, smiling
- Stocky, buck-toothed, myopic, delicate
- Obedient, passive, stolid, docile, unquestioning
- Servile, subservient, submissive, polite
- Mystical, inscrutable, philosophical, stoic.

The news behind the news

How many of these "news facts" do you know?

1.   *The news is big business, not a community service.* Many news organizations don't want to offend their audiences—or their advertisers. So they may "bury" a story in the middle of the paper.

Advertisements pay the bills at most newspapers. Subscriptions and newsstand sales account for a smaller and smaller portion of a daily newspaper's revenues. TV news programs depend on advertising, too.

2.   *The news reflects the views of the owners.* The news media are often owned by huge corporations. The stories that appear, what "slant" (point of view) they are given, what reporters are assigned to cover them, how "deep" in the newspaper or broadcast a story is placed (in other words, how far from the front page or opening moments)—all of these things and more depend on the opinions and agendas of the owners.

Most major U.S. daily newspapers belong to a handful of corporations. In 1993, The New York Times Corporation bought the *Boston Globe*. How do you think that might affect the *Globe*? What are the pros and cons of two papers—or more—being owned by the same company?

3.   *Journalists and reporters can and do make mistakes.* They have daily deadlines, frequently research and write several stories at once, are only as accurate as their sources, and have to contend with time and space limitations.

For instance, even major TV news stories last only about five minutes on the nightly national news, less on the local news because local broadcasts include sports and weather segments. What you see may reflect hours, even days of research and interviews condensed to fit in with other stories. A long and detailed story may become a single "sound bite" lasting only a few seconds.

In newspapers, a 15-minute interview may be reduced to a single sentence. Whole paragraphs of newspaper stories sometimes are cut to make the story fit around advertisements. That's one reason why reporters put the least important facts at the end of a story. If the story needs to be shortened, the most important facts stay in.

Consider the source

To make the most of the news, you need to consider where it comes from and decide whether the source is credible, or believable.

Cable television networks like C-Span, CNN, and Court TV offer viewers the chance to hear many sides of many issues, including the role of the media, a regular topic on CNN's "Reliable Sources" and PBS's "Roundtable." C-Span features speeches by politicians and other leaders so you can make up your own mind about where they stand.

After giving a speech that was broadcast on C-Span, Louis Farrakhan, the controversial leader of the Nation of Islam, invited his audience to read the next day's papers and compare the media's versions of what he had said to what they had just heard him say.

Court TV features excerpts from trials whose outcomes have a profound effect on American society. The first trial of the Los Angeles police officers charged with using excessive force when arresting Rodney King, the William Kennedy Smith rape trial, and the Clarence Thomas confirmation hearings, in which law professor Anita Hill accused the Supreme Court nominee of sexual harassment, were among the major events featured during 1991–1993.

These networks and others like them also regularly feature debates and roundtable discussions on current events and the issues they raise. But here, too, consider the source. Who do the speakers and guests work for? What is their personal investment in the outcomes they advocate? What companies sponsor the programs? What are their special interests?

How to have a nose for news

If you want the facts about our diverse culture, you need to learn to recognize distorted and slanted news coverage. Here's how:

1.   *Don't believe everything you read in newspapers or see on the TV news.* If possible, check the facts for yourself. See if you can find the same story reported in three or four different sources (news magazines, newspapers from different cities). Read the stories and compare the findings and conclusions.

2.   *After you read or see a story, try to determine what's been left out.* Every story has two sides. Were both sides reported? Was one side shown in a more favorable light than the other?

3.   *Understand that each media source serves a different function.* To really understand an event or an issue, don't limit yourself to just one source.

■ Television news can only sketch the outlines of most stories. Supplement what you see there by watching special reports and documentaries that the national networks (ABC, CBS, NBC, PBS, CNN, and others) often produce following important events.

■ Daily newspapers with more space to give stories (sometimes several column inches) and time to research them (sometimes a week or longer) often add important and interesting details— people with various viewpoints describing an event, background information on organizations and people involved, facts about similar events or issues—that help put things into perspective.

■ Magazines sometimes have weeks or longer to work on stories. They might add numerous photographs, charts and graphs, and details elaborating on facts and events covered more briefly in newspaper accounts.

TIME OUT

Analyze your local newspaper. Start with the first page and work your way through. As you read the stories, answer these questions:

1.   How many of the people mentioned in the stories are white males? How can you tell?

2.   How many are criminals? How are they identified? For example, does one story tell about "four men" who robbed a convenience store, while another tells about "a young black male" who stole a car?

3.   How many are victims?

4.   How many are females? How are they identified—as homemakers? lawyers? feminists?

5.   How often do members of minority groups appear, and in what contexts? Are they professionals making important contributions to society? Experts on various subjects? Witnesses to crimes? Criminals? Victims?

6.   How often do members of minority groups appear in negative stories as opposed to positive stories?

7.   How much space is devoted to each person mentioned? How high in the story does his or her name or contribution appear?

8.   Are most of the reporters male, or female?

9.   Do male reporters and female reporters cover different kinds of stories? For example, do male reporters cover the crime stories, while female reporters cover the human interest or feature stories?

Do this for a couple of weeks and keep lists of what you find. Then analyze your findings. Do patterns emerge? What do you think they mean? Consider writing a letter to the editor about your findings and conclusions.

If you live in a small town, you may want to compare your local paper with a big-circulation paper like the *New York Times, Los Angeles Times, Chicago Tribune, Washington Post,* or *Houston Chronicle.*

• • • • • • • • • • • •

THINK ABOUT IT

TALK ABOUT IT

1.   Imagine one day waking up to find that racism, sexism, prejudice, and discrimination don't exist anymore. Write a front-page newspaper story (or group of stories) about the effects on various groups of people and institutions. Then think ahead 2–3 months, when this phenomenon isn't news anymore. What will you write about then?

2.   Some publications and news programs pay for interviews with people involved in scandals or crimes. What impact could paying a source have on the story?

3.   Pick a controversial current event and compare the way it's covered by different newspapers, magazines, and TV shows. How many, if any, sensationalize the event?

4.   Where do you draw the line between news and what the Navajo call "gossip"?

Creative Writing Class Brings Students Together

*"This class doesn't pour things into us.
It teaches us how to pour things out."*

Galileo student

Galileo High School stands at the busy intersection of Van Ness Avenue and Bay Street near San Francisco's Fisherman's Wharf. The relaxed noontime scene at Galileo portrays the ethnic separation so familiar on the campuses of so-called "integrated" schools and reflects our racially divided society.

Asian American guys wearing baggy black sweaters and white turtlenecks, their bangs swept up high above their foreheads, hang out on the corner eating Chinese food from take-out containers. Shouting and laughing, two black girls in cheerleader outfits chase a black boy wearing a San Francisco Giants baseball cap. Inside, in a long hall, two large groups of girls—one immigrant Indian, the other Chinese American—sit against opposite walls eating brown-bag lunches. A narrow patch of hallway divides those inward-facing circles; no communication crosses that invisible line.

But lines drawn between races, ethnicities, and academic skill levels are crossed in the creative writing and poetry class taught by Judy Bebelaar and Poet-in-Residence Katharine Harer. In this class, serious attention to writing, communication, and self-expression are combined with a major emphasis on building a strong sense of community among students who would not otherwise have the opportunity, support, or courage to come together.

NITA WINTER PHOTOGRAPHY

Members of the Galileo High School creative writing class

As student Felix Jones says, "This class doesn't pour things into us, it gives us room and encourages us and teaches us how to pour things out."

Twice a week, students listen to and write verses meant to reveal the human beings behind the skin colors in the classroom. The teachers read from works by writers of different races, cultures, and nationalities.

Antoinette Easley—president of the Black Student Union, varsity basketball player, and poet—steps forward to practice presenting her poem, "This is My Town," for a National Poetry Week Reading: *"Black as midnight and skin as dry as the Mojave desert, selling their bodies to get a piece of the devil's white powder. This is my town."* Three students performing with her echo the refrain, *"This is my town."* Voices from various corners of the class agree that the group needs to put more into the reading. So, in the next run-through, Antoinette exaggerates, stretching some words, shortening others, and putting long pauses in unpredictable places. Soon everyone is laughing hysterically. The backup "singers" posture like rappers, spinning and strutting to the rousing applause that acknowledges the improvement in the performance.

Teacher Judy Bebelaar asks Mary Chav, a Cambodian student, and Matthew Fong, a Chinese student, to read a philosophical discussion about lies, a work they have written together. Their style is quieter and more contemplative than that of Antoinette and her chorus. In the comments afterward, the other students demonstrate an appreciation for the differences.

Which is what it's all about.

Adapted from a profile by Laurie Olsen, director of the California Tomorrow Immigrant Students Project, that appeared in *Embracing Diversity: Teacher's Voices from California's Classrooms* (San Francisco: California Tomorrow, 1990). Used with permission.

Getting along in a
changing world...

Rethinking My Prejudices

"Middle Eastern men ride camels; how could they possibly know anything about cars?"

As the author of a book about prejudice, bias, racism, and sexism, I may know a lot about those issues and how they affect individuals, families, and communities. But I still have a lot to learn, too. Or maybe I should say a lot to *un*learn.

I've lived most of my life in the South, where gas station attendants, mechanics, and station owners wear uniforms, sometimes overalls in rural areas. When I saw smoke pouring out of my car's exhaust one day, I pulled into the first gas station I found. A man in his fifties wearing overalls was pumping gas while three young, expensively dressed Middle Eastern men watched and chatted.

I got out of my car and headed for the man in overalls. Meanwhile, one of the other men opened the hood of my car. All three peered at the engine, talking as they poked and jiggled parts inside. One yelled at me, "You need a new gasket! This one is completely ruined. How did this happen?"

"Pretty rude behavior," I thought, "especially from a stranger." I even felt threatened. I'm not used to being yelled at. Besides, I wanted to see the man in the overalls. Why were those Middle

Eastern men looking at my car and asking me questions? Who did they think they were?

As it turned out, they were the owners of the gas station, and they knew a lot about cars—a lot more than the man I had assumed was the owner.

So much for my stereotypes of Southern service-station owners…not to mention my stereotypes of well-dressed Middle Eastern businessmen.

When I looked back later on the incident, I realized that my reaction had been triggered by several old stereotypes. Like "Middle Eastern men ride camels; how could they possibly know anything about cars?" And "Middle Eastern men sell rugs, they don't own gas stations." And even "You can't trust Arabs."

When I learned those ideas, maybe 30 years ago, they may have represented popular beliefs about Arabs at the time. Meanwhile, the world had changed…but my stereotypes hadn't. Neither, as it turned out, had the stereotypes of a lot of other people.

During the Persian Gulf War, U.S. politicians and the media portrayed the Iraqis as bloodthirsty, immoral warmongers. Radio disc jockeys and talk-show hosts raved that the U.S. should "nuke the Iraqis," even though only a small percentage of the population was involved in the war. Popular T-shirts showed a camel-riding Arab framed in the crosshairs of a rifle sight.

The Anti-Arab Discrimination Committee reported a significant increase in violence directed at Arabs. Even children picked up on the "patriotic" behavior that would otherwise have been considered racist and unacceptable. One teacher described a three-year-old playing war, explaining that his jets were "bombing the brown people, the bad guys."

Rather than trying to understand Saddam Hussein's behavior in the context of Iraqi culture, which in some cases values honor more than life, most people accepted the popular diagnosis—that he was a "madman." Very few reports mentioned that American politicians sometimes approached Hussein in ways that made it impossible for him to "save face" (maintain his honor), a crucial aspect of masculinity in many cultures.

I don't mean to sound as if I supported Hussein and his actions in Kuwait. All I'm saying is that there's more to this situation than meets the eye. The average American was not well-informed about American and Iraqi history and their different ideas about patriotism, leadership, duty, and morality and how those ideas influenced the events leading to and surrounding the Persian Gulf War.

The 1993 bombing of New York's World Trade Center added fuel to our national anti-Arab sentiment, since the suspects were from Egypt, Palestine, Kuwait, and Jordan, all countries included in the Arab world. A suspected plot to blow up the United Nations Building also involved Arabs.

When I read about American reactions to the Gulf War, the World Trade Center bombing, and the U.N. Building plot, it was easy for me to see that many of these reactions were based on prejudice, like my reaction to the men who checked my car. What if newspapers and magazines had to print a positive story for every negative story about Arabs and other minorities? What impact do you think this would have on stereotypes and prejudice?

CHAPTER 4

Does Race Really Matter?

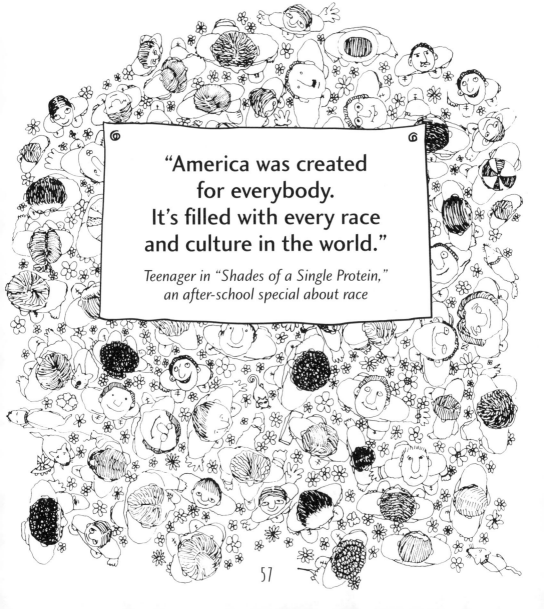

"America was created for everybody. It's filled with every race and culture in the world."

Teenager in "Shades of a Single Protein," an after-school special about race

Everybody's an "other"

On a television talk show, a young Los Angeles writer who has just won an award for her work talks about her family background. Her parents are Chinese and Lebanese. She was born in America and writes short stories, including one about how it feels to fly down the freeway at 70 miles per hour, the wind in her hair, singing along with Tracy Chapman's hit song, "Fast Car."

In an Italian grocery in New Orleans' French Quarter, two young women with Asian features chatter away in Australian-accented English. They are trying to decide whether to buy some English work boots they saw earlier at a nearby mall, or to use the money for three new CDs by American rock groups.

Is the writer with Lebanese and Chinese parents an American? What would it be like to celebrate American, Lebanese, and Chinese holidays? To eat a variety of foods from all three countries—falafel, mu shu pork, hamburgers (which actually came from Hamburg, Germany)? To grow up with multi-ethnic relatives, speaking a variety of languages?

Could the young women in New Orleans be Americans? Considering their Asian features, why do you think they speak with Australian accents?

These two incidents illustrate the growing diversity in today's society and the so-called "race mixing" (intermarriage) that drives white supremacists crazy and starts them raving about protecting the purity of the white race. But, according to scientists, there hasn't been a pure race, white or otherwise, for more than 100,000 years.

Today there are as many as 2,000 racial variations. "Pure" white and "pure" black are nonexistent and, chances are, even most white supremacists have "mixed" ancestry. And things are getting more complicated: *Harper's Index* estimates that there has been a 223 percent rise in intermarriage among ethnic groups since 1970. As this continues, putting people into neat little boxes marked "black, Asian, Hispanic, German, Native American and 'other'" will become impossible, because only "other" will really be accurate.

The new U.S. census form offers more than 100 ethnic background choices, including Peruvian, Armenian, Spanish Basque, and French Basque.

BANDAGES AND CRAYONS OF MANY COLORS

- For people of color, new Multiskins offer adhesive bandages in dark, medium, and light brown.

- Crayola has responded to today's ethnic diversity by giving us more colors to choose from. For years, they made a single standard "Flesh" crayon—a pale pinkish color. Today there's "My World Colors," a collection of 16 "skin, hair, and eye colors" from around the globe. It includes a black crayon, a white crayon, and 14 shades in between.

- A reader of *New Moon* magazine (see pages 145–147) is trying to convince Crayola to change the "Indian Red" crayon to "Native American Red." But isn't that a stereotype, too, since Native Americans don't really have red skin? And since it brings to mind slurs like "redskin"?

Theories about race

Some scientists speculate that more than 100,000 years ago there were just three races: Mongoloid (Asian), Negroid (black), and Caucasoid (white). We still use those labels, however inaccurately, on birth certificates, marriage licenses, college applications, and other official forms.

Today the whole concept of race is undergoing a thorough re-examination. Some current theories suggest that Mongoloids, Negroids, and Caucasoids developed different physical characteristics to adapt to the climates where they lived.

For instance, Mongoloids may have developed larger eyelids than the other two races because they came from mountainous country with strong winds, and large lids helped keep dust from blowing in their eyes. Although their eyes are the same shape as the eyes of Caucasoids and Negroids, the lids give people the impression that Asians have "slanted" eyes. Because their eyes look less open than the eyes of blacks or whites, this has led to the misconception that Asians are mysterious and unknowable—or, in other words, inscrutable, sneaky, and sly.

Actually, the "slanted" eyes of Mongoloids are singled-lidded eyes. Caucasoids and Negroids have double-lidded eyes with a deep crease that follows the top of the eyeball. (Asians don't have this crease, but some are undergoing plastic surgery to give them double-lidded eyes so they'll look "more American.")

Size may be another adaptation to the cold mountainous regions where the Mongoloid race originated. Asians tend to be small and compact, the ideal shape to retain body heat.

In Africa, where the Negroid race evolved, the sun was very hot, so Negroid people may have developed long, lean bodies to deflect heat. Black skin also has more of a brown chemical called *melanin*, which all races have in different amounts. Melanin makes Negroid skin dark and protects it from burning.

Asians have more *carotene* in their skin, a substance which gives it a yellowish cast, and whites have more *keratin*, a clear chemical. All three races have some of each. Different mixtures of the three chemicals account for the hundreds of skin colors.

More than 300 years ago, anthropologists "invented" the concept of race as a convenient way to categorize the people they studied. The lightest skins, they believed, belonged to Northern European Caucasoids who evolved in what we now call Scandinavia. Since sunlight is scarcest in those regions, humans needed very little melanin in their skin. As with the Mongoloid race, stocky physiques developed as an adaptation to cold.

Obviously, there are exceptions to all of these "types," and many modern anthropologists reject the three-race theory. In fact, many reject race as a way to classify humans, period, because of the thousands of variations within each category.

According to one educator, eye color and skin color are determined by the same chemical, so it makes just as much sense to judge people by eye color as skin color.

Does race really matter?

It might be nice, and it certainly would be convenient, if we could say that race doesn't matter. But it matters very much in many ways, both negative and positive.

At best, race gives a person individuality, a sense of belonging, a unique way to understand and experience the world. The dizzying array of races makes culture exciting, a continual learning adventure.

SKJOLD PHOTOGRAPHS

At worst, race can provoke discrimination and violence from prejudiced people. Where tolerance is absent and people are harassed, humiliated, or killed because of their color, race can become a source of shame.

Race is used to determine eligibility for college scholarships and grants as well as what majors and courses a college offers. For instance, the course catalog for the University of California at Berkeley, one of the most ethnically diverse colleges in the U.S., lists Chicano, Asian, Native American, and Afro-American studies, among others. Courses offered include "Survey of Native American Tribal Government," "Mythic Tribal Literature," "Black Political Life in the U.S.," "Law in Chinese Society," and "Buddhism and Contemporary Society."

There's even great diversity among ethnic groups and races. The Native American professors listed in Berkeley's catalog belong to the Choctaw, Chippewa, Potawatomi, Siksika, and Blackfoot tribes.

The government uses sizes of ethnic populations to decide how much money to spend on important social services for those groups—affordable medical clinics, literacy programs, low-income housing, and access to tests for diseases that affect individual races, such as sickle cell anemia for blacks. Theoretically, the larger the ethnic group, the larger the funding.

Changing ethnic identity

With more than 2,000 ethnic variations, can you always tell who's Asian? Hispanic? Lebanese? Can you take a person's word for what he or she is?

Not necessarily. Because there's so much competition for admission to good colleges and to get good jobs and promotions, people aren't always honest about their race. According to the *San Francisco Examiner:*

■ In the San Francisco Unified School District, about 150 parents each year change their children's racial or ethnic designation. Sometimes this reflects a change in self-identity, such as when a child learns to take pride in belonging to a specific "minority" group. But at other times the change may help a student get into a better school, where one ethnic group is given preference over others in an effort to balance the overall ethnicity of the student body.

Several years ago, the University of California at Berkeley began admitting more students of color in an attempt to reflect the ethnic makeup of the diverse community it serves. Now some white students complain that it's almost impossible for them to get in. But if a white student has Asian or Hispanic ancestry—or claims to—his or her chances will be better.

How could you prove your ethnicity? Just because someone doesn't "look Asian" doesn't mean he or she isn't. Pretend you can't find your birth certificate. Would a blood test provide proof? A DNA test? How about a family history or genealogy?

The *San Francisco Examiner* further reported that:

■ In the San Francisco fire department, some white firefighters have conducted elaborate research about their ancestors, hoping to find one who will qualify them as part Hispanic and improve their chances of getting a promotion.

■ Throughout the United States, the number of people claiming to be Native American increased by 40 percent over the last decade, some hoping to benefit from federal programs for Native Americans.

Not everyone who proudly proclaims their racial or ethnic heritage after years of trying to blend in has an ulterior motive. Over the past five to ten years, America's awareness and acceptance of our country's multicultural makeup have grown—and so have the numbers of Americans who are standing up to be counted as Chicanos, Arab Americans, Native Americans, and others.

Racial "science" or science fiction?

Theories about race are interesting, but in the wrong hands they can be dangerous. During the 18th century, Petrus Camper, a Dutch anatomist and painter, was one of many intellectuals who believed that external physical features reflected a person's intelligence and morality. This theory was accepted as scientific fact for more than 100 years after Camper's death.

To Camper and his fellow intellectuals, muscular, evenly proportioned, athletic Greco-Roman man represented the ideal type. They believed that blacks were related to monkeys and represented an evolutionary stage between apes and white men. Women were left out of their theories altogether.

In 1792, physician Benjamin Rush, one of the signers of the Declaration of Independence, published a paper explaining his theory that blacks suffered from an extreme form of leprosy. In essence, he was saying that blackness was a disease, and his "scientific observations" were based on prejudices of his time.

This kind of thinking reappeared in Hitler's obsession with destroying the "dirty Jews." Because he believed that Jews spread germs and disease "like rats," he ordered the "extermination"—a word typically used to describe killing pests like rats, roaches, and termites—of millions of Jews.

During Hitler's rule, German educators promoted a "science" called "raciology" which supported Hitler's belief that Jews were ignorant and subhuman. For a Holocaust education project sponsored by Facing History and Ourselves, a national education and teacher training organization that helps students examine racism, prejudice, and anti-Semitism, a man named Frank recalled his humiliating experiences as a 12-year-old Jewish schoolboy in a "raciology" class in 1933. The teacher ordered Frank to the front of the room as an example of "the Jew," then pointed out Frank's features, explaining that they marked him as an "inferior human being" while the features of a blond-haired, blue-eyed classmate represented the "ideal human." For months, Frank's classmates so harassed him for being a "dirty Jew" that he begged his parents to let him leave school. In 1934, he dropped out.

TIME OUT

Imagine standing in front of your class while your teacher—someone you look up to, someone who has power over you—tells your classmates that you are no better than a diseased animal. In fact, your teacher explains, you are an "inferior specimen" who should be exterminated.

How do you feel? What do you do? What do you say to your class-mates? To your teacher? To your family? Think about it, then write a paragraph about what you would say to one person you know.

● ● ● ● ● ● ● ● ● ● ● ●

As recently as the 1950s, some anthropologists proposed that brain size and skull shape were directly related to intelligence. The anthropologists, who were white, concluded that whites had the largest brains and blacks the smallest. Their theories also "proved" that women were less intelligent than men because their brains were smaller.

Beliefs such as these—that some people are "naturally" igno-rant and inferior because of race and/or gender, while others are "naturally" intelligent and superior—have led to human rights abuses throughout history. Here are a few examples (you can prob-ably think of others): the Holocaust, enslavement of African Americans, Cambodian genocide, the internment in concentration camps of Japanese Americans and Italian Americans during World War II, female infanticide (killing female babies because they are "less valuable" than males), denying women the right to vote…and on and on.

Would you be surprised to learn that several prominent public figures—including a college professor, a former Louisiana state representative, and a police officer, to name just a few—express similar opinions today?

■ In 1991, Dr. Leonard Jeffries, head of the black history depart-ment at the City College of New York, lost his job for teaching that white people are genetically inferior to black people. Jeffries' lectures also included accusations that Jews are united in a conspiracy against blacks and whites.

■ David Duke, former Louisiana state legislator, former national leader of the Knights of the Ku Klux Klan, and founder of the National Association for the Advancement of White People, ran for Louisiana governor in 1990. Duke calls himself a "racialist" rather than a racist. According to his definition, a racialist does not hate people of other races. He just believes that there are biological differences between races (mainly that blacks are inferior to whites) and wants to protect the "purity" of his race. In 1989, Duke was selling anti-Semitic literature from his legislative office near the State Capitol, and during the same year the phone book listed his home telephone number for the Ku Klux Klan.

■ Los Angeles police sergeant Stacy Koon, one of the officers charged in the Rodney King case, insists that he is not a racist. Yet, in his memoir, he tells a story about shooting a black man, then joking that the man would survive because blacks "are too dumb to go into shock." He also used the term "Mandingo"— an offensive reference to black slaves—to refer to King, a black Los Angeles motorist who charged that police used excessive force in arresting him.

1.   What do you think the term "melting pot" means? Does it accurately describe what happens when immigrants come into an established majority culture?

2.   Doesn't the First Amendment (freedom of speech) give public figures like David Duke and Leonard Jeffries—as well as all Americans—the right to spread their ideas about the superiority of their races? In Duke's case, doesn't it give him the right to tell others his belief that the Holocaust never happened?

3.   Read about the First Amendment. Decide if you think that firing Dr. Jeffries went against his constitutional right to free speech.

4.   David Duke claims that he's a "racialist," not a racist. What do you think of this argument? Also, Los Angeles police officer Stacy Koon has asserted publicly that he's not a racist. What do you think of this in light of the remarks that have been attributed to him?

Getting along in a
changing world...

"Said, Yo! Said, Oy Vey!"
Black-Jewish Rap Group
Promotes Racial Understanding

"Me and my boys overcame the hype
As we broke through each other's stereotype
We don't murder, we don't steal
We work hard to buy a meal
We don't do drugs to get our spirits flowin'
Like to keep our brain cells alive and growin'
I ain't into money and I love to play ball
It's true my friend, one God made us all
So as you go through life with your sisters and brothers
Remember, you can't judge a book by lookin' at the cover."

Dr. Laz & the CURE

Combine a Jewish educator and a black Baptist minister, both with a strong desire to bring together a divided community, throw in some enthusiastic, idealistic black and Jewish youngsters who like to rap and hip-hop, and you've got Dr. Laz & the CURE, maybe the world's first black-Jewish rap group.

Their motto is "Increase the Peace," and their method is communication. As one of their raps proclaims:

> *"Communication*
> *Across the nation*
> *Let's all sit down and have a conversation."*

David Lazerson with members of the CURE

© TEQUILA MINSKY 1992

The "Increase the Peace" Hebrew-English logo shows two clasped hands, one black, one white.

Dr. Laz & the CURE (for Communication, Understanding, Respect, Education) didn't come along a moment too soon—not long after the 1991 summer riots in Brooklyn's Crown Heights neighborhood threatened to destroy the established but troubled black-Jewish community.

The longtime tension between the two groups erupted into violence when a black youth was killed by a car driven by a Hasidic Jew, and a Hasidic youth was stabbed in revenge. New York Mayor David Dinkins was hit in the head with a bottle when he came to the neighborhood to plead for peace. A police car was overturned and set on fire.

The rage and chaos lasted for two months. Repairing black-Jewish relationships could take years, even with the help of dedicated groups like Dr. Laz & the CURE.

High school teacher David Lazerson and Reverend Paul Chandler decided to try to get the two groups thinking about racial harmony and then get them talking—to each other. So, with the help of some neighborhood kids, they started rappin'—first all over town, then on "Donahue" and other national talk shows, National Public Radio, and even in Congress. They have a rap/rock video in the works and a second recording on the way.

At a performance for students from Brooklyn's 19 high schools, according to the *Boston Globe*, "the group had young people dancing in front of the stage, swaying their hands in the air, and singing along to the words of 'Funky Racists.'"

> *"Funky racists, funky, funky racists.*
> *Funky racists try to keep us all confused.*
> *Funky racists, funky, funky racists.*
> *They go around spreading lies about blacks and Jews."*

Most of all, Dr. Laz & the CURE has enlightened a community that has coexisted for years without knowing much about each other. T.J. Moses, a CURE dancer, had never even talked to the Hasidic Jews he passed everyday on the street. "I didn't know anything about them," he says. "I was kind of scared."

Yudi Simon, a Hasidic teen group member, also admits he was ignorant and frightened. "I couldn't look at a black person and think of him as a person. I'd look at them and think of them as someone out to hurt me."

A black youth said that the sight of a group of Hasidic boys walking toward him at night made him nervous. The astonished Jewish youth said they thought *they* were the only ones who were afraid of strangers.

Once the two groups were a little more comfortable with each other, the questions flowed. The black youngsters wanted to know why the Hasidic all wore dark clothes and "beanies" (yarmulkes). The Jewish youth asked about dreadlocks and reggae music. "How come all you guys look alike?" a black youth demanded. The reply? "A lot of us feel the same way about you."

Reverend Paul Chandler, the black Baptist minister who helped Lazerson start Dr. Laz & the CURE, asked them to look at each others' feet. "All the Jews wear shoes," he said. "All the blacks wear sneakers. So *you* got a uniform—and *they* got a uniform, too. See?"

Compiled with information from *Buffalo* magazine, World of Lubavitch, the *Boston Globe* and *The Washington Post*.

CHAPTER 5

Watch Your Language

"There's still a prejudice
against people who
don't sound the way
white people sound."

Attorney in a job discrimination suit

71

Speaking in stereotypes

"Chere, he was downtown eatin' a muffaletta, not lookin'
where he was goin', and he tripped on the banquette
and fell. You should see the hickey on his elbow! "

If that makes sense to you, you're probably from New Orleans, a city with at least three distinct dialects. "Chere" is a French-derived word meaning "dear," "darling," or "honey." "Downtown" means "down river" (as opposed to "uptown," which means "up river." The river is the Mississippi). A "muffaletta" is a sandwich served by local groceries and cafés especially in the French Quarter. A "banquette" is a sidewalk. A "hickey" in this context means a big bump or bruise.

Here's the translation of our story:

"Honey, he was in the French Quarter eating a sandwich,
not looking where he was going, and he tripped on the sidewalk
and fell. You should see the bruise on his elbow!"

The original story was in "Y'at," a dialect that reveals important clues about the speaker's social class, education, and career. Someone familiar with New Orleans speech and accents can use these clues to make assumptions about the speaker. In other words, speech offers another way to stereotype people.

In general, the more one's speech varies from Standard English, a kind of unaccented English spoken by white middle-class Americans, the more likely the speaker will be discriminated against.

▲▲▲▲▲▲▲▲▲▲▲▲▲▲▲▲▲▲▲▲▲▲▲▲▲▲▲▲

I PLEDGE A LESSON...

Bette Bao Lord, best-selling author of *Legacies: A Chinese Mosaic*, came to the United States from Shanghai, China, when she was eight years old. This is what the Pledge of Allegiance sounded like to her: *"I pledge a lesson to the frog of the United States of America, and to the wee puppet for witch's hands, one Asian, in the vestibule, with little tea and just rice for all."*

From *Newsweek*, July 6, 1992. Reprinted with permission of Bette Bao Lord.

You are what you speak

At least, that's what some people think.

In New Orleans alone, you'll hear these three variations of English:

- "Y'at," the white "downtown" English (from "hey, where y'at?," a version of "hello, how are you?");
- white "uptown" English, spoken by the residents of the expensive and elegant Garden District; and
- black English.

"Y'at" resembles speech you might hear in Brooklyn, New York. A New Orleans resident who speaks "downtown" English might say:

> *"Dahlin', some touris' done ax me today if I was fum Brooklyn, and 'at ain't dah fois time neider."*

Can you translate?

"Uptown" is a more drawling dialect, closer to the way most non-southerners think all Southerners speak. It's also closer to Standard English than "downtown" or black English. Its speakers are usually wealthy, well-educated professionals—bankers, lawyers, doctors—and their families. Many are descendants of the city's American founders, who earned huge fortunes in sugar, cotton, and shipping. A New Orleans resident who speaks "uptown" English might say:

> *"Ah nevah knew yo-ah fathah was an actah."*

Black English is a high-speed, slang-rich dialect spoken all over the United States. Someone speaking black English might say:

"'Sup, homes? You funna go see that brother?
He well lame man, serious lame."

Translation:

"What's up, friend? Are you getting ready to go see that guy?
He's uncool, man, very uncool."

Speakers of black English and white "downtown" English complain that people assume they're ignorant and "low-class" because of the way they talk. Their job prospects may be limited to blue-collar jobs or service jobs. Employers might pass them over for promotions, especially if the new job involves more contact with the public. Teachers might give better grades to students who speak "uptown" English because that dialect is associated with intelligence.

For their part, blacks and "Y'ats" think that "uptown" talkers sound snooty. "Y'ats" have formed a "Y'at Power" movement to celebrate their distinctive dialect. Supporters can be seen at New Orleans Saints football games waving signs asking "Who Dat?," a reference to the fact that not long ago, not many people had ever heard of their beloved team.

All three groups are convinced that they talk just fine and the other two groups are the ones with "funny accents."

By the way, if you ever visit New Orleans, you might hear a *fourth* dialect: Cajun *patois*. The Cajuns are descendants of French Canadians who live in Louisiana's bayou country. Their *patois* is a blend of 17th-century French and idioms from the English, Spanish, German, Indian, and black settlers who also came to southern Louisiana. Cajun is mostly spoken by people over 40 who live west of the city, but you'll often hear Cajun terms in the unique Louisiana dance music called *zydeco*.

Do you know anyone who "talks funny"? Is that person's speech or accent really "funny," or just different?

Make a list of your friends—best friends, good friends, and people you just hang around with. Now think about how you all sound when you talk. Does anyone speak with an accent that stands out from the group?

● ● ● ● ● ● ● ● ● ● ●

Bilingual English

To avoid discrimination, many black Americans have become bilingual, speaking two languages—black English in their neighborhoods and Standard English at work, in classes, and in other multi-ethnic settings.

Blacks who speak Standard English in their neighborhoods risk the criticism —and ostracism—of their peers. In "Yeah You Rite!," a film by Louis Alvarez about the way people speak in New Orleans, a black teenager admits that her friends tease her because she enunciates more clearly than they do and uses less slang. "People think I'm trying to be cute," she says.

If a black professor tried to teach multi-ethnic classes in black English, she probably would be looking for another job soon. What kind of response do you think a political candidate who spoke black English would get from voters?

Do you know any whites, Hispanics, Asians, or people from other ethnic backgrounds who speak a second English dialect? Do you talk the same way with your friends as you do with your parents, teachers, and other adults?

SPRECHEN SIE DEUTSCH?

Many Amish children grow up speaking German and only learn English when they start school. Since the Amish have little contact with the outside world and don't watch TV, listen to the radio, or go to movies, they sometimes have trouble pronouncing English words even though they can read and understand them.

Combination languages

Hawaii holds the honor of being one of America's most multi-cultural states. According to the National Public Radio series "The Prejudice Puzzle," 60 percent of the islands' residents are people of color, descended from settlers who came from the South Pacific Islands, China, Portugal, Japan, Korea, and the Philippines.

Like many African Americans, Hawaiians speak a kind of bilin-gual English. Their local dialect is *pidgin*, a mixture of two or more languages, created by early Asian immigrants who worked on the pineapple and sugar cane plantations. Today's Hawaiian teenagers speak a new version of pidgin, a combination of so-called "planta-tion" pidgin, black English, and California "valley speak," a dialect that originated among wealthy Southern California teenagers and spread across the United States.

But, like black English and "Y'at" in New Orleans, pidgin is considered to be the language of the lower classes. Hawaii's governor, John Waihee, speaks pidgin and praises it as "a door into local values." The Hawaiian press apparently doesn't agree, because reporters sometimes "correct" the governor's speech in news stories.

DO YOU SPEAK GULLAH?

Gullah is a hybrid language spoken by former slaves and their descendants living on the Sea Islands of South Carolina and Georgia. Here are two Gullah sentences and their translations:

> *"Shishuh tall pass una."*
> ("Sister is taller than you.")

> *"Una-chil' naymnyam fufu an t'ree roll-roun', but 'e ain't been satify."*
> ("The girl ate mush and three biscuits, but she wasn't satisfied.")

Do you speak Gullah? If you've ever said the words "cooter" (tortoise), "gumbo" (a soup thickened with okra), "juke" (as in jukebox), and "voodoo" (witchcraft), the answer is yes. These are all Gullah words.

The number of Gullah speakers is declining as the Sea Islands are being developed and turned into vacation resorts. But the language is still spoken by the remaining "Geechees"—a word for people who speak Gullah.

Language barriers

Until the late 1950s, Hawaiian students were legally segregated according to how well they spoke Standard English. Most whites ended up in the English Standard schools, while most students of color went to schools where pidgin was favored.

James, a half-Hawaiian meteorologist with a college degree and 20 years of experience in his field, speaks with a soft, melodious Hawaiian accent. In 1986, he submitted an audition tape to the National Weather Service (NWS). He was turned down for a job for the weather channel on the radio because the NWS judged his speech "poor" and his delivery "unclear and hesitant." The NWS hired a white man instead, and James filed a federal job discrimination suit.

The attorney who represented James called the incident "rank prejudice." "They frankly wanted someone on the radio who sounded white," he said, "because a few people complained. And because there's still a prejudice against people who don't sound the way white people sound." The U.S. District Court judge didn't agree; James lost. When he appealed the decision, he lost again.

CU VI PAROLAS ESPERANTO?

International languages, sometimes called universal languages, are ways for people to communicate even when they normally speak different languages. During the Middle Ages and the Renaissance, Latin was an international language. Scholars who normally spoke French, German, or English could get together and converse in Latin. Swahili serves the same purpose in Africa, where more than 50 languages are spoken.

Since the 17th century, there have been several hundred attempts to create universal languages. The most popular by far is a language called Esperanto, a word that means "hopeful."

Unlike Latin, which evolved naturally, Esperanto is an *artificial* language. The man who made it up was Dr. Ludwig L. Zamenhof of Poland. He first presented his new language to the public in 1887. Today there are anywhere from one to fifteen million fluent Esperanto speakers in the world. Most are in Eastern Europe, but there are many in Japan, China, and elsewhere. Several countries transmit radio broadcasts in Dr. Zamenhof's language, and many books have been translated into it.

The vocabulary of Esperanto comes from Latin, Greek, Italic, and Germanic languages. The grammar is based on European languages, greatly simplified. The spelling is phonetic.

Here are a few examples of phrases in Esperanto:

"Mi estas de Usono."
("I come from the United States.")

"Ne tro rapide, me petas."
("Not too fast, please.")

"Saluton! Kiel vi fartas?"
("Hello! How are you?")

Sticks and stones

"I always hear people say, 'Sticks and stones may break my bones, but words will never hurt me,'" says Detective Lieutenant Bill Johnston of the Boston Police Department, Community Disorders Unit. "Tell that to a little girl who's just been called a nigger."

We use language to describe and define other people, so we need to choose our words with care. Especially when describing people, we need to use respectful words that acknowledge their humanity and individuality. Just about everybody knows that slurs ("spic," "faggot," "nigger," "redneck," "beaner") are insulting and insensitive—and in some cases against the law, if they are used to threaten violence. But what about words and phrases we use everyday without thinking about them?

- Have you ever called somebody an "Indian giver"? We all know what it means: a person who gives you something, then takes it back. But what does it have to do with Native Americans?

- Have you ever used the phrase "Jew down"? When you're buying something, it means that you managed to get the seller to lower the price. When you're selling something, it means that someone talked you into selling it for less than you originally wanted. What negative stereotype about Jews does this phrase perpetuate?

- Have you ever taken part in a "Chinese fire drill"? You're riding in a car with friends when you pull up to a stop sign. Suddenly everyone jumps out of the car, runs around like crazy, and gets back in the car again. Sometimes two or more people try to crowd into the same seat. Why call this a "Chinese fire drill"? Do you think that when Chinese people have a fire drill, they run around like crazy? This phrase implies disorganization and chaos. It's insulting to Chinese and Asian American people.

■ To "get your Irish up" means to become irrationally angry. That's because all Irish people are hot-tempered and quick to anger…right?

■ Have you ever seen a race car driver do a "Polish victory lap"? The winner drives once around the course…backwards. Why is this called a "Polish victory lap"? Supposedly because Polish people are too dumb to drive in the right direction.

■ Do you know a "gal Friday"? A woman—perhaps a secretary or an executive assistant—who performs a variety of duties? Lots of women consider "gal" (or "girl") a demeaning term. (Would you call an adult male "boy"?) And "Friday" refers to a character in the novel *Robinson Crusoe*. In the story, Friday is a reformed cannibal who waits hand-and-foot on Crusoe, his white master. When a businessman calls a woman his "gal Friday," he usually means it as a compliment. Is it?

People who would never say "chink" (Chinese), "Christ-killer" (Jew), or "redskin savage" (Native American) use phrases like "Indian giver" and "Jew down" without giving them a second thought. What are some other prejudiced, insensitive words and phrases we use without thinking?

Try to think twice about what you say…maybe three times.

Did you hear the one about…?

Overheard at the YMCA: "Did you hear that the recession killed more Jews than Hitler?" It's not as direct as name-calling or insulting phrases, but it's just as powerful and maybe more dangerous because it's presented as a "joke." Most people are familiar with the stereotype that all Jews are rich enough to invest in the stock market. The "joke" implies that the recession "killed" (bankrupted) millions of Jews.

Presuming that some Jewish investors did lose money in the recession, can we really compare this to being murdered by the Nazis? In fact, six million Jews died during the Holocaust, a dark and devastating time in world history. Many individuals and families still carry Holocaust-related physical and psychological scars. The "joke" trivializes their horror.

If you're Jewish, how does this "joke" make you feel? How does it make you feel if you're not Jewish?

There's an unspoken understanding that if "it's just a joke" or if someone is "just kidding," it's okay to make offensive, insensitive remarks. But at least one black teenager doesn't agree…not after some white teenagers who were drinking and making jokes about blacks at a party ended up assaulting him. Neither do the families, friends, and colleagues of eight lawyers who were gunned down in their San Francisco law office in 1993. After the lawyers were killed by a disturbed client of their law firm, several of their coworkers appeared in television interviews, saying that they believed jokes and stereotypes about lawyers as greedy, ruthless, and power-hungry contributed to the violence.

Playing dumb

What do you do when you hear someone tell a racist, sexist, homophobic, or otherwise biased and prejudiced "joke"? Staying silent implies agreement, but speaking up can make you the next target. There's another alternative: playing dumb.

Meg Daniel, a graduate of the National Conference "Anytown USA" human relations camp, explains how this technique works: "If you just get up on your soap box, nobody's going to listen to you. So, if someone tells a racist or sexist joke, you just pretend you don't get it. Then they have to explain it—explain what makes it funny.

"The more they try to explain, the dumber it sounds. You basically let them do the talking, so it's hard for them to feel like you're attacking them. They end up feeling stupid, and you really don't have to do anything. It's perfect. And they may think twice about doing it again, since you've really put them on the spot."

CULTURAL ETIQUETTE

According to *Cultural Etiquette: A Guide for the Well-Intentioned* by Amoja Three Rivers:

- "A large radio/tape player is a boom-box, or a stereo, or a box, or a large metallic ham sandwich with speakers. It is not a 'ghetto blaster.'"
- "It is ethnocentric to use a general term such as 'people' to refer only to white people and then racially label everyone else."
- "Words like 'gestapo,' 'concentration camp' and 'Hitler' are only appropriate when used in reference to the Holocaust."
- "Race is an arbitrary and meaningless concept. Races among humans don't exist."

Excerpted with permission from *Cultural Etiquette: A Guide for the Well-Intentioned* by Amoja Three Rivers, © 1990, 1991. Available from Market Wimmin, Box 28, Indian Valley, Virginia 24105.

THINK ABOUT IT **TALK ABOUT IT**

1.   If you lived in New Orleans and you spoke black English or "Y'at," would you feel comfortable going into a fancy French Quarter restaurant? If you spoke white "uptown" English, would you feel free to approach a group of classmates who were speaking black English?

2.   Imagine what it would be like to live in the United States if you couldn't speak English at all. Or let's say you could speak it, but only a little, and you had to repeat everything three or four times before people understood you. How would you feel?

3.   Has anyone ever made fun of the way you talk? How did you feel? What did you do?

4.   Do you think that people in a multicultural society should all have to speak the same language? Why or why not? Try to come up with reasons for both points of view.

5.   When was the last time you heard a racist, sexist, or otherwise biased joke? What did you do or say?

6.   When Amoja Three Rivers says, "Race is an arbitrary and meaningless concept. Races among humans don't exist," what do you think she means?

Getting along in a changing world...

Building Bridges: Memphis Camp Unites Black and White Teens

"I'm going to change. I'm going to start communicating."
High school student

"Used to be every time I'd see a white person I'd say 'hello,' they'd say 'hello,' and we'd just keep on walking," says Markell Newsom, whose Memphis high school has 10 whites and 1,056 blacks. The way Newsom figured it, whites didn't want to talk to him and he saw no reason to talk to them.

But those days are over now, he says. "I'm going to change," he promises. "I'm going to start communicating."

What made the difference? A program called Bridge Builders. Founded in 1988 by Youth Service, an Episcopal social service agency in Memphis, Bridge Builders brings together high school students from the city's mostly black public schools and mostly white private schools for two years of leadership and human relations training.

Bridge Builders begins with a week together the summer between students' sophomore and junior years. Three of the seven afternoons are devoted to community service—sorting cans for a food bank, stuffing envelopes for the Heart Association, whacking weeds at a senior citizens' center, and other activities. The rest of the time is spent writing speeches and playing games that emphasize interdependence.

NEWHOUSE NEWS SERVICE

Blindfolded Bridge Builders learn to depend on one another

Then, for the next two years, the students meet monthly, work on other community service projects, and get back together for another camp their second summer. The goal is to develop a rapport among the young blacks and whites who in a generation will be running the city.

One of the purposes of Bridge Builders is to make participants feel comfortable talking about race, stereotypes, prejudice, and discrimination. They read, talk, and role play: "You're the black mayor of Memphis. You need to annex a white suburb to build the tax base and raise the money you need to keep your promises to help the poor. But annexation will put enough whites on the voter rolls to defeat you in the next election. What do you do?" (The rough consensus in one group was to win a second term, then annex.)

Scott Moore, who just finished his two years with Bridge Builders, says he can no longer tolerate the racist views of his old friends at school. "It really hit me when I got back," he says. "They'd go through the play-by-play of a Bulls game. They think Michael Jordan is at the left hand of God. But they can follow that with a racist story or joke." Still, he says, "they don't consider themselves racist because they'll say, 'I like my maid, she's great.'"

Adapted from "Building bridges: In divided Memphis, camp brings together black and white teens," by Jonathan Tilove, Newhouse News Service, August 2, 1992.

CHAPTER 6

The First Universal Nation

"History is the fable
agreed upon."

Napoleon

History books: The whole story?

Many of the authors you are reading (or will read) in school—Walt Whitman, William Faulkner, Ernest Hemingway, Emily Dickinson, and Virginia Woolf, to name a few—were descended from white Europeans or European Americans. So were many of the authors whose books you grew up on, including Dr. Seuss, A.A. Milne, E.B. White, Maurice Sendak, Judy Blume, Kenneth Grahame, and Beverly Cleary.

Unless your history books are the latest editions, they may not contain accurate information about the contributions of Native Americans, African Americans, Hispanics, Asians, or women. If they do include those groups, the books may perpetuate stereotypes about them.

- Did you know that during the Westward expansion almost one in three cowboys was black? Or that some cowboys today are Jewish? Or that some "cowboys" are "cowgirls"?

- Do you believe that all "Indians" were bloodthirsty savages who murdered innocent white soldiers and settlers? You may not have learned—or you may have learned only recently—that Native Americans attacked soldiers and settlers because they were trying to protect the land where they had lived for thousands of years. When their land was taken anyway, they were confined to reservations, where many Native Americans still live today. (Did you know that some Native Americans are also Jewish?)

- Did you know that not all slaves were black? Or that there are slaves today in dozens of countries around the world? Slavery still exists in Moslem countries, even though it's forbidden by the Koran, the sacred text. Children are often sold by poor parents to work as domestic servants, and the children of female slaves also become slaves. In South Africa, many young people illegally cross the border from famine-stricken Mozambique, looking for work in Johannesburg. But once they're in South Africa, they have no rights, unless they have work permits. Most don't, so the young women are often sold into prostitution, slavery, or forced marriages, and the young men are forced to work for meager pay on farms or construction crews. According to *Cultural Etiquette: A Guide for the Well-Intentioned,* the word "slave" comes from the Slavic people of Eastern Europe. Author Amoja Three Rivers writes: "Because so many Slavs were enslaved by other people (including Africans) especially in the Middle Ages, their very name came to be synonymous with the condition....Virtually every human group has been enslaved by some other human group at one time or another."

Here are some interesting facts about African Americans that you probably won't find in your history books:

- In 1883, Jan Ernst Matzeliger invented the machine that made possible mass-produced shoes and created thousands of jobs.
- The famous Lewis and Clark expedition of 1803–1806 included a black man named York who was invaluable to the expedition.
- In 1885, Sarah Goode inventing the folding cabinet bed. In 1892, Sarah Boone invented the ironing board.
- The first man to reach the North Pole wasn't Admiral Peary but Matthew Henson, the navigator for Peary's expedition.
- In 1887, A. Miles invented the elevator.
- Daniel Hale Williams, a black cardiologist, performed the first successful open heart surgery.

"Valuing Diversity," an award-winning seven-part video series (San Francisco: Griggs Productions, 1990) points out that:

- Germans brought the Groundhog Day tradition to the United States.
- The traffic light was invented by an African American.
- The windshield wiper was invented by a woman.
- Chicago was founded by a Haitian.
- Vitamins were discovered by a Polish immigrant.
- An Arab American invented the ice-cream cone.
- A Russian American stuffed the first teddy bear.

For more fascinating facts about the contributions that African Americans, Asian Americans, Hispanic Americans, Native Americans, and European Americans have made to the United States, see *The Peoples Multicultural Almanac: America from the 1400s to the Present* (Rochelle Park, NJ: The Peoples Publishing Group, Inc., 1994). Check your local library or contact the publisher at:

> The Peoples Publishing Group, Inc.
> 12 Overlook Avenue
> Rochelle Park, NJ 07662
> Toll-free telephone: 1-800-822-1080

MEET SARAH WINNEMUCCA

Most history books note that Pocahontas, a member of the Powhatan Indians of Virginia, saved John Smith, an English colonist, from being executed by her father. Pocahontas later became a Christian and married a white settler, which may have helped to assure her place in history.

Most history books *don't* mention Sarah Winnemucca, even though she was an important Native American leader during the late 1880s, when few Indians and few females were allowed a voice in political affairs. A Paiute of the Nevada tribe, Sarah—her Indian name was To-me-to-ne, or "Shell Flower"—devoted her life to improving the lives of Native Americans.

After teaching herself to read and write and to speak English and Spanish, this remarkable woman played a vital role during the 1878 Bannock Indian uprising against the U.S. Army, risking her life to deliver a message that changed the course of events. Later she succeeded in persuading government officials to let the Paiutes return to their home reservation, after they had been forced to leave because the Army believed they had collaborated with the Bannocks.

Before her death in 1891 at age 47, Winnemucca established two schools for Indian children and lectured across the United States on behalf of her tribe and others. Her 1883 autobiography, *Life among the Paiutes: Their Wrongs and Claims,* was one of the first books by a Native American.

PHOTOGRAPH AND BIOGRAPHICAL INFORMATION COURTESY OF THE NEVADA HISTORICAL SOCIETY, RENO, NEVADA

Sarah Winnemucca

The good guys wore white... and were white

White European American historians, predominantly male, first recorded the history of our nation, and their version has only been challenged during the past decade. Until recently, our culture was reflected back to us through literature also written by white European Americans, again predominantly male. Naturally, the heroes of history and literature were the same race and gender as the storytellers. People of color—black, Hispanic, Native American, Asian—had to play the villains, servants, or sidekicks.

- Could racial stereotypes explain the association of white with good and black with evil, as in old Westerns (and even some recent action movies), where the bad guys wear black?

- Could they explain the association of yellow (the color most often used to describe Asian skin) with cowardice, as in "You're a yellow-bellied coward" and "You've got a yellow streak a mile long?" Why is journalism that exploits, distorts, or exaggerates the news called "yellow journalism?" When Asian American TV news veteran Connie Chung calls herself a "yellow journalist," she turns a slur into a pun and lessens its power to cause pain.

Because American history has been distorted, many Americans have a very one-sided view of the world they live in. But minority groups are speaking out and demanding recognition for their contributions. At the same time, they are insisting that the truth be told about such "heroes" as General George Custer, whose troops massacred thousands of Native Americans before being killed at Little Big Horn River. They are blowing the whistle on the wealthy railroad barons who opened the Western United States to expansion by exploiting thousands of Chinese laborers. While the railroad barons were getting richer, the Chinese were doing the back-breaking work of blasting tunnels through mountains and laying track.

During recent years, historians have concluded that even Columbus wasn't such a great guy. After all, everything was fine, at least as far as the native peoples were concerned, until the Italian explorer "discovered" America, bringing with him contagious diseases and other trappings of "civilization." As Amoja Three Rivers writes in *Cultural Etiquette*, "Columbus didn't discover diddly-squat. There were millions of Native Americans who had known for countless generations that what they were living on was land, and where it was—was right here."

Some textbook publishers are working to present a less biased version of history, one that includes the contributions of the many diverse peoples who made America.

HISTORY'S TOP 10

According to *The 100: A Ranking of the Most Influential Persons in History* by Michael Hart (Secaucus, NJ: Citadel Press, 1993), these are the ten most important people in human history:

1. Mohammed
2. Isaac Newton
3. Jesus Christ
4. Buddha
5. Confucius
6. St. Paul
7. Ts'ai Lun
8. Johann Gutenberg
9. Christopher Columbus
10. Albert Einstein

They weren't all white men, but they were all men. Do you know what their contributions were? Their nationalities?

More than two-thirds of the people on Hart's list of 100 come from Europe and North America. Only two women are listed: Queen Isabella I of Spain (number 65) and Queen Elizabeth I of England (number 94). Dr. Martin Luther King, Jr., a revered American civil rights leader who won the Nobel Peace Prize, made Hart's "Honorable Mentions and Interesting Misses" list.

Where on the list would you put Dr. King? In the top 10? The top 20? Make a Top 10 list of your own.

TIME OUT

- Name three books you've read during the past year by people of different religions, people of color, gay men or lesbians, people with disabilities, and/or people from different cultures. If you haven't read any, maybe it's time to get started. Reading is one of the best ways to learn about other people. Ask a librarian for suggestions.

- Start a multicultural book club. Ask a librarian, literature or social studies teacher, or someone at a local bookstore for guidance and recommendations. (You'll also find a list of recommended titles on pages 167–168 of this book.) Everyone in the group could read the same book each time, or you could agree on a subject (life as a person in a wheelchair, as a Muslim woman, as a Rastafarian, as a homeless person), each read a different book, and report back to the group on what you have learned. You might invite people with firsthand experience (a person in a wheelchair, a Muslim woman, etc.) to visit your group.

- Make up your own 21st-century reading list reflecting contemporary and future cultural diversity.

● ● ● ● ● ● ● ● ● ● ● ●

Politics: Changing for the better

Since the Revolutionary War (and before), our political leaders—the people who make vital decisions about our lives—have been white males. As one Hispanic student asked on a radio program about race, "If America is a melting pot, why are there so few people of color in government? How can you represent me when you don't know me?"

But that's changing, too. Local, state, and federal governments are beginning to reflect the fact that the American "mainstream"—the majority values in our society—is fed by diverse tributaries. That means the unique views and concerns of women, Hispanics, homosexuals, and other cultural groups are more likely to be heard and respected.

Consider this list of elected and appointed officials, all serving at the time this book was written:

- Roberta Achtenberg, Assistant Secretary of Housing and Urban Development and a lesbian

- Ruth Bader Ginsburg, a Supreme Court Justice and a Jew

- Sandra Day O'Connor, the first female Supreme Court Justice

- Jocelyn Elders, Surgeon General of the United States and an African American (she succeeded Antonia Novella, the first female and first Hispanic Surgeon General)

- Barney Frank, a senator from Massachusetts and a homosexual

- Willie Williams, Los Angeles police chief and an African American

- California senators Diane Feinstein and Barbara Boxer

- Carol Moseley Braun, an Illinois senator and an African American

- Texas Governor Anne Richards

- Colorado senator Ben Nighthorse Campbell, a Native American

- Donna Shalala, Secretary of Health and Human Services , a Lebanese American woman

- Minneapolis, Minnesota, Mayor Sharon Sayles Belton, an African American woman.

TIME OUT

Name three important people in your town or school from diverse, nontraditional backgrounds. They don't necessarily have to be politicians. Other influential groups include school boards and faculties, human rights organizations, neighborhood associations, and arts and humanities groups.

● ● ● ● ● ● ● ● ● ● ● ●

A nation of nations

America always has been a diverse nation. In fact, poet Walt Whitman described it as a "nation of nations" almost 150 years ago, when your great-great-great grandparents were your age. What do you think Whitman meant by these words?

By the 1800s, people from all over the world had followed their dreams of freedom, equality, and prosperity to the United States. In addition to Native Americans and early English settlers, "Americans" included Lithuanians, Russians, Italians, Greeks, Scandinavians, and Nova Scotians, as well as men, women, and children from China, Ireland, France, and other countries.

According to Michael Kronenwetter, author of *United They Hate: White Supremacist Groups in America,* most of the early explorers and settlers of North America were *not* pale-skinned Protestants from England. "The Spanish were the first to colonize most of the New World, including Florida and the American Southwest," he writes. "It was Hispanic Roman Catholics, not British Protestants, who established the first Christian churches in North America, as well as the first theaters and schools, and even the first American university. The French were the first to explore most of the rest of what is now the United States."

Strangers in a new land

Immigrant children at Ellis Island, New York, during the early 1900s

In 1892, a young Irish girl became the first immigrant to pass through the Ellis Island "processing station" in New York Harbor. From 1892–1943, Ellis Island was the gateway into the United States for millions of immigrants. At the processing station, they were checked for contagious diseases, filled out applications for admission to the U.S., and were often given new Americanized names if the customs officers couldn't pronounce their native names.

For many immigrants, milk and meat had been scarce at home. Some had never seen white bread and butter. Many recalled being overwhelmed by the sight of the huge pitchers of milk and platters of fish and meat, white bread and butter set on the long dining hall tables at Ellis Island.

VOICES FROM THE PAST

"We lived through a famine in Russia and we almost starved to death…. My mother said she wanted to see a loaf of bread on the table and then she was ready to die. So, you see, we lived through so much before we came here that Ellis Island was a blessing." Rose, 10, Russian

"Around four o'clock on Sunday afternoon they hustled us into a courtyard where there were chairs set up…. We watched a magician, singing, comic acts, most of which we did not understand. When I was a little bored, I turned my head and stayed that way, because behind us was New York harbor with all the skyscrapers…my first glimpse of Manhattan. I was mesmerized." Joseph, 11, Hungarian

Imagine being one of those children, forced by poverty, starvation, oppression, or persecution to leave your country for a strange land.

- You'd be leaving behind your friends and relatives, knowing you might never see them again. Who would you miss most?

- You could only take what you could carry. What would you take?

- You'd be sleeping and eating with strangers who spoke dozens of languages you couldn't understand. You'd be surrounded by people, yet isolated. And you'd never be sure exactly what was happening, what to do, or how to get what you needed. How would you communicate?

Stephanie Auxila, a young girl who came to the U.S. from Haiti in 1987, after her family suffered two machine-gun and hand-grenade attacks, remembers: "I could not understand people, so I could not do what I was told. So I always went to the end of the line and watched what others did first, and then I imitated them."

Special thanks to the National Park Service Ellis Island Immigration Museum, a part of the Statue of Liberty National Monument, for the historical information and oral histories.

TIME OUT

■ Think about your family. What countries did your ancestors come from? Do you have pictures of them? Do you know stories about them? If not, ask your parents and grandparents to tell you what they remember. Then ask yourself, "How am I like my ancestors? How am I different?" You may want to write down some of your thoughts, discoveries, and insights.

■ Put together a family history. Begin with the story of how your family came to America or, if you're Native American, with the history of your tribe. You can learn a lot about how historical events affected the lives of your parents and other relatives and how American culture has changed over the decades. This will also give you a new appreciation of the family members and elders you interview, which is part of what *Respecting Our Differences* is about—developing a greater appreciation and understanding of others.

■ The "Family Folklore: Interviewing Guide and Questionnaire," published by the Smithsonian Institution Folklife Program, is a good guide for first-time family historians. The eight-page brochure is available from:

> Superintendent of Documents
> U.S. Government Printing Office
> Washington, DC 20402

■ The 100-page book, *Family Folklore*, is a collection and discussion of how to preserve your family stories, traditions, photographs, and memorabilia. Write to:

> Folklife Programs
> L'Enfant 2100
> Smithsonian Institution
> Washington, DC 20560

● ● ● ● ● ● ● ● ● ● ● ●

Different is normal

Today's increasing diversity is most obvious in schools. From 1990 to 1993, 120,000 children from 167 countries entered the New York City Public School System. That's enough students to populate a city the size of Santa Fe, New Mexico, or Sioux City, Iowa. That's more than three times as many countries as the U.S. has states.

At Garfield Elementary School in Revere, Massachusetts, about 50 percent of the students are Southeast Asian, especially Cambodian. Every new child is immediately paired with a "buddy." Buddies are responsible for helping new children find their way around during the first week—introducing them to friends, sitting with them at lunch, showing them where they need to go.

Does your school have a buddy program? If not, why not propose one? You might suggest that it last much longer than a week.

Language is one of the most frustrating and difficult barriers for immigrants to overcome, and it is one that leads to many misunderstandings. When a French student with minimal English skills visited Alabama and ordered a glass of milk in a small-town café, the waitress answered, "We don't serve beer." A ten-year-old Hungarian-Canadian student living in Los Angeles was teased by his classmates every time he said "third," because he pronounced it "turd."

Even professional interpreters don't always get it right. A Los Angeles agency which specializes in translations (everything from Romanian birth certificates to Arabic love letters) once printed a church newsletter that turned "our Lord in heaven" into "our guy in the sky."

In "Immigration Today," a story published in *National Geographic* magazine, 15-year-old Wenny Cui recalled how she felt about coming to America from China without knowing any English: "When we first came, I cried and cried. My father cry with me, because we don't know English. Not even A-B-C." Today Wenny speaks clear English and does well in school. But she has another problem; call it "freedom shock." Wenny comes from a country where people have limited choices, even about the number of children they may have. So she's a little overwhelmed by the United States, where choices seem endless. "How, with so many possibilities," Wenny wonders, "do you decide in America what you want to be?"

Reach out and touch...everyone

Here are three ideas that will help you to start learning more about the world around you and practicing tolerance:

1.   *Be willing to fail.* Think about all the things you know how to do—play a musical instrument, use a computer, turn cartwheels or do handstands, use the telephone, read. You probably "failed" at all those things lots of times before you finally mastered them.

Instead of saying "I failed at…" or "I couldn't do…" or "I couldn't figure out…," try saying "I practiced…." For example: "I practiced that really hard computer program…," "I practiced my handstands…," "I practiced reading a challenging book…." Keep practicing and you'll be rewarded with new skills and knowledge.

2.   *Be willing to start wherever you are with whatever knowledge you have.* Your desire to learn will make up for whatever you don't know yet.

Listen to your negative self-talk—the voices in your head that try to discourage you by saying "I'll embarrass myself…," "I'm not sure what I want to accomplish…," "I don't know where to begin…." Then change those "can'ts" to positive messages like "Why should I be embarrassed about wanting to be a better person?" "I'll figure out each new goal as I go along, and eventually I'll have a clear idea of what I want to achieve." "Reading this book will help me figure out how to get started."

3.   *Turn stumbling blocks into stepping stones by learning to tolerate discomfort.* Learning more about your world and becoming more tolerant may be uncomfortable at first. But if you keep trying and don't give up, you'll actually end up feeling *more* comfortable with yourself and others, and you'll find yourself enjoying new experiences, making new friends, and having new adventures. Fear of discomfort may be worse than the actual discomfort itself, just as dreading a test may be worse than taking it.

1.   What do you think Napoleon meant when he said, "History is the fable agreed upon"?

2.   How would you define history for someone who doesn't know what it is?

3.   How would American history be different if most historians had been Native American women?

4.   What have you learned during the past few years in history class that contradicts what you learned in grade school?

5.   How would you answer Wenny Cui's question, "How, with so many possibilities, do you decide in America what you want to be?" If Wenny were still in China, how would she choose a career? Do some research on China—and especially women in China—to find an answer.

Getting along in a changing world...

Glide Memorial Church: Where Services Are Celebrations

"At Glide we believe that the true church stays on the edge of life where the real moans and groans are."

The Reverend Cecil Williams

At first glance, there might not seem to be much worth celebrating in San Francisco's Tenderloin District, home to many of the city's prostitutes, drug addicts, and poor minorities. But, as a sign at the neighborhood's Glide Memorial Church proclaims, "Celebration is when you come to the conclusion that LIFE after birth and before death is more important than life after death."

So on Sunday mornings, Reverend Cecil Williams and his ever-changing multicultural congregation gather for a "celebration," Glide-talk for church service. No matter how early you get there, you'll probably find two long lines of people—one waiting for a seat or standing space in the sanctuary, one waiting for a meal. For many years, Glide has been feeding more than 1,000 people a day, not just with meals but also with the spiritual nourishment that brings a community together and gives each member a sense of belonging.

Glide Memorial Church Sunday celebration

Reverend Williams calls his congregation an "extended family" and embraces users of crack cocaine, victims of early childhood sexual abuse, and people with AIDS as well as the middle class and well-to-do. A typical Sunday may find a famous black poet sitting next to a crack addict with AIDS, sitting next to a white Financial District power broker, sitting next to a Latino family who gets by on the income from a small restaurant they own. Next to them may be a gay couple talking to their newly arrived Cambodian immigrant neighbors who haven't yet found jobs, even though both parents are skilled professionals.

As he writes in his book, *No Hiding Place*, Reverend Williams believes that the problem with many churches is that "folks settle in, get comfortable, and build...walls to protect themselves from anyone who thinks or looks differently than they do. At Glide we believe that the true church stays on the edge of life where the real moans and groans are."

Reverend Williams came to Glide in 1963 and went to work immediately crusading for civil rights. He took a planeload of San Franciscans to Selma, Alabama, to march for voting rights with Dr. Martin Luther King, Jr., and formed Citizens Alert, a support group for blacks, homosexuals, and prostitutes.

Today he strides up and down the aisles—when they're not packed with churchgoers—reminding the members of his congregation that each of them is as good as anybody else. When the Sunday celebration is over, everybody leaves with that hopeful message in mind and, instead of the traditional preacher's handshake, a heartfelt hug from the messenger.

CHAPTER 7

New Definitions

"There are more extraterrestrials on TV than Latinos and Asians."

Latino writer Rick Najera

The "average American"

Look through some magazines and see if you can find some examples that fit your stereotype of an "average American." Now look for pictures that look like you. If, like Latino writer Rick Najera, you don't fit the norm—if, for example, you are paraplegic, overweight, Amish, albino, Rastafarian, Asian American, Native American, Arab American, or otherwise "different"—you may have trouble finding people who look like you in magazines and also in newspapers, catalogs, on greeting cards, and on television, whether in programs or commercials.

According to the *New York Times*, the absence of blacks in ads for an Arlington, Virginia, housing development cost the owner $850,000. Citing the Fair Housing Act of 1968, plaintiffs in a lawsuit argued that the development's use of exclusively white models over a five-year period had sent the message that blacks were not welcome.

If the advertising industry wants to reach the "average American," we need to see many more people of color, nontraditional families, people in wheelchairs, homosexuals, and members of diverse religious groups on billboards, in advertisements, and in commercials.

Some companies are starting to get the message. Some examples you might have seen:

- A commercial for Kellogg's Corn Flakes features a hearing-impaired teenager signing about the cereal as someone off-camera interprets.

- In a commercial for Oreo cookies, an Asian boy and a European American boy enjoy a snack together.

- Ads for Saturn cars feature a Latino woman and a group of Latino musicians.

- A Wal-Mart commercial features a customer in a wheelchair.

- A male model who frequently works for the Ralph Lauren company and a reporter on a popular network news show both use wheelchairs.

■ An AT&T ad shows a young woman ordering pizza with a TDD (Telecommunications Device for the Deaf) that's sort of a cross between a telephone and a typewriter. The user types in her order and a hearing operator "translates" it for the pizza restaurant. The operator, who also has a TDD, types in, "Your order should be there in 30 minutes," and the words appear on the young woman's TDD screen.

If you've ever seen magazine ads or billboards for Bennetton clothing, where models of many nationalities, skin colors, and religions are shown together, you already have an idea of what the future will look like—in advertising and in fact.

TIME OUT

■ Create an advertising campaign for the 21st century. You might design collages featuring people of color, multiracial families, people in wheelchairs, Asian Americans, a single-parent family headed by a man, and other cultural groups not often portrayed in ads today.

■ Suggest that your class or your school—or perhaps all the schools in your city—do a "21st Century People" poster project. Ask human relations groups, community service organizations, or a local newspaper to sponsor a city-wide competition, with prizes and recognition (in the newspaper, on television) for the top ten entries.

● ● ● ● ● ● ● ● ● ● ● ●

The white minority

For at least a century—maybe longer—the "average American" has been a white, middle-class, able-bodied heterosexual male. But not for much longer. Soon, for the first time in many generations, the white Americans whose views, values, and customs have dominated our culture will be a minority group. Already in large cities—for instance, Los Angeles—people of color outnumber whites. Nationally, according to a Census Bureau report released in 1993, racial and ethnic minorities form the majority in more than 2,000 U.S. cities, towns, and counties.

As a result, today's so-called "minority groups" can look forward to being better represented in government, the media, and other important institutions and organizations. The most influential writers, artists, scientists, etc. of the 21st century probably will look very different from the ones we know today. So will magazines, catalogs, greeting cards, and television programs and commercials.

The high school and middle school reading list of the near future should include names like:

- Isabel Allende (Chilean)
- Maxine Hong Kingston (Asian American)
- Toni Morrison (African American)
- Kate Braverman (Latina)
- Oscar Hijuelos (Cuban)
- Gus Lee (Asian American)
- Elie Wiesel (Jewish)
- Gabriel Garcia Marquez (Colombian)
- Umberto Eco (Italian)
- Louise Erdrich (part Native American)
- Milan Kundera (Czechoslovakian)
- Nadine Gordimer (South African)
- Gita Mehta (Asian Indian).

TIME OUT

Think of three specific examples of how the shift in population in the United States already is affecting (or soon will affect) the following:

- government

- large corporations

- universities

- medical research facilities

- news and entertainment media

- other traditionally white-dominated institutions.

Look through newspapers or news magazines for stories on this issue. Write down some of the most interesting and/or surprising facts you find.

● ● ● ● ● ● ● ● ● ● ● ●

Who's a family?

The shift in racial composition isn't the only major change taking place in the United States today. The family isn't just Mom, Dad, and two kids anymore. Instead, there are more extended families (several generations living together), large adopted multiracial families, grandparents raising their grandchildren, single-parent families, gay-parent families, families with no children, and divorced families. These groups challenge our stereotypes of what a family is and should be.

If a couple doesn't have children, can they call themselves a family, or are they "just a couple"? A generation or so ago, people got married primarily for the purpose of having a family. Is that still true? For many people, marriage still means family. But many married couples choose not to have children, and many people (couples and singles) have children without getting married.

If the parents of two teenagers are divorced, are the four still a family even though the parents aren't husband and wife anymore? What about "blended families," which include two parents, children from previous marriages, and new children?

The 1959 *Webster's Dictionary for Boys and Girls,* a dictionary your parents may have used when they were children, defined "family" this way: "1. All the people who live under one head and in one house. 2. All the people who are descended from the same ancestor; a clan or a tribe. 4. A group of closely related people, as parents and their children."

Here's how 12-year-old Paul Gienger of Streeter, North Dakota, defined "family" for the National Public Radio special, "Class of 2000: Family Stories": "When I think of family, I think of many things. I think of home-baked meals, some good, some bad. I think of people who might take you somewhere if you want to go. I think of a place you can come if you are having a bad day, and not do a thing." Notice that Paul didn't mention anything about who's in his family and what their relationships are to each other. He focused on how his family feels to him.

Six-year-old Anthony and his brother sometimes stay with their aunts or grandmothers for several days at a time. Their parents both work, and they have a large network of relatives who can help out. Anthony can't imagine a family where there are only two parents.

If you were writing a dictionary, how would you define "family" to reflect contemporary society? For instance, is there a "head of the family" anymore? Is there just one "head"? Parents today often share the responsibilities that come with being the "head" of a household. And what about the kids of divorced parents? They don't usually live in one house all the time. Does that mean they're not part of a family? Or do they have two families?

According to Dallas O'Brien, an 18-year-old from St. Francis, Kansas, "It will probably get to where you're weird if you live with both your biological parents. It's too bad that everyone can't have two parents, and those of us who do should enjoy it more."

What about the families you see on television? In the movies? How do they compare with the family described in the 1959 dictionary definition? Think about "The Brady Bunch," "The Simpsons," "Cosby," "Roseanne," "Home Improvement," "Full House," and other shows (or the shows you watch most often).

What about the families you know? Do they fit the definition? What about *your* family?

Our changing neighborhoods

Our neighborhoods reflect the changes taking place in our culture and our families. When Anthony's parents moved into their neighborhood a few years ago, their neighbors were mostly white heterosexuals of European descent. Now they are Asian Indian, Vietnamese, Korean, and, like Anthony, African American. Several are gay and lesbian. One has albinism. About a dozen mentally impaired neighbors live in a nearby group home. There's also a Palestinian extended family which includes a grandmother and two adult daughters in their thirties.

A new Catholic student center recently opened about a block from a Victorian house used as a mosque by Muslim university students. Two houses down from Anthony lives the son of Mormon missionaries. Walk a few blocks in one direction and you can sign up for Polynesian dance classes. Go about the same distance in the other to learn the Cajun two-step.

Ask Anthony what he thinks of his Asian Indian neighbors' colorful saris or the two women who hold hands, and he'll probably shrug and tell you how much he likes to ride his bicycle or play on the slide and teeter-totter in the park across the street. Fun is his top priority, not cultural diversity. But, whether he realizes it or not, growing up in his neighborhood is giving Anthony a head start when it comes to adapting to our changing culture. He's already used to being around all kinds of people. Why shouldn't he feel just as comfortable and flexible in the future?

TIME OUT

What about your school, neighborhood, and city? What kinds of changes have you seen in recent years? Ask your parents or older neighbors to tell you about the way things used to be. How have they dealt with the changes?

• • • • • • • • • • • •

Getting to know your neighbors

People don't always deal with change in positive or constructive ways. For instance, some of Anthony's white neighbors ignore him and his family and other people of color in the neighborhood. The retired white railroad worker next door to Anthony makes rude remarks about the Lebanese family across the street. The Asian Indians, Vietnamese, and Koreans keep to themselves.

The neighborhood I live in is as diverse as Anthony's. We have a neighborhood May Fair every year. Reggae, folk, and hip-hop groups perform, Hindu dance demonstrations are held, and vendors sell ethnic food. A huge flea market lures everybody who likes a bargain. But that's just one weekend a year. Can you think of other ways our neighborhood could celebrate our differences?

What about *your* neighborhood? Do you have chances to meet, mingle with, and enjoy learning about people from other cultural groups? Or does each group tend to stay isolated and apart from the others? If that's the case, how can you help to change it? What opportunities exist for people to get to know one another? What new opportunities can you create? What about organizing a community project?

1. Are Anthony's mentally impaired neighbors who live in a group home a family? Why or why not?

2. Do you have a mental image of an "average American"? If you do, write a paragraph about him or her before you read any further.

3. Read your paragraph and ask yourself: Is your "average American" male or female? How old? What does he or she look like? Where does he or she live? What does he or she do for a living? For fun? Finally: Where did your image come from?

4. How will life be different for white Americans when they are no longer the majority? How will it be different at school? At work? At home? In their communities?

Getting along in a changing world...

The Village of Arts and Humanities: A Paradise in the Inner City

"It's all rubble, but if you look at it from a different angle, it's all resources."

Lily Yeh, Executive Director
Village of Arts and Humanities

Normally, you'd have to go to a museum or fly across the ocean to find Ethiopian angels, African architecture, Chinese gardens, and Islamic courtyards. But in North Philadelphia, one of the nation's most impoverished neighborhoods, in what six years ago was an abandoned lot filled with rubble, residents have created all those things—and much more.

Guided by the vision of Taiwanese artist Lily Yeh, children and adults from the community built Ile-Ife Park (Ile-Ife means "House of Love" in the Yoruban language of Nigeria). A walk through the park is like a visit to wonderland. There are dragon-shaped mosaic benches, angel and phoenix murals, flowers, a community vegetable garden, and a children's garden.

The park grew into a larger project, the Village of Arts and Humanities, which offers children's art programs (including a fabric arts class), adult literacy classes, writing workshops, martial arts instruction, and African dance classes to almost 200 participants. A master builder from New Mexico came to help the children build an adobe horno, a traditional Pueblo outdoor oven for roasting corn and other foods. Future plans include a housing rehabilitation program, a community kitchen, and a children's newsletter.

Scenes from the Village of Arts and Humanities

THE VILLAGE OF ARTS AND HUMANITIES

THE VILLAGE OF ARTS AND HUMANITIES

THE VILLAGE OF ARTS AND HUMANITIES

**Scenes from the Village
of Arts and Humanities**

THE VILLAGE OF ARTS AND HUMANITIES

"My mom never worries when I'm here," says Destiny Williams, 9, who lives nearby in a neighborhood once called "The Badlands" by the *Philadelphia Inquirer*. "She always sees me doing things."

Children and adults from the neighborhood performed "It Pulls It All Apart," a play they developed from interviews with neighborhood residents and performed outdoors at the Village. "Big Man" Maxton, a former drug addict turned artist whose involvement in the park helped him recover from a long addiction, recalls opening night: "Most of the people who came were attracted to the lights. Then they saw that (the play) was about their own lives, their trials and tribulations. These are people who had never been to a theater before. And they were there again the next evening."

In another play, "Children's Dreams and Lives," children revealed their inner lives through angels in masks, ghosts dancing in graveyards, and a ritual procession.

The Village also provides space and support for a Narcotics Anonymous group and holds annual summer, harvest, and Christmas festivals as times of neighborhood giving and sharing.

Nicky Garlington, a 12-year-old working on the Village vegetable garden, wanted to put barbed wire around the lettuce to keep people from stealing it. Yeh's husband Stephen Sayre assured Nicky that even if someone stole the lettuce, the work she was doing was still worthwhile. After all, it had brought together a diverse group of children and adults and given them a way to use their talents, imagination, and intelligence to create community and magic in the midst of alienation and despair. Yeh agrees, saying, "It's important that we learn to make commitments despite the constant threat of loss."

To find out more about the Village, write or call:

    The Village of Arts and Humanities
    2544 Germantown Avenue
    Philadelphia, PA 19133
    Telephone: (215) 225-3949

CHAPTER 8

Stereotypes and Scapegoats

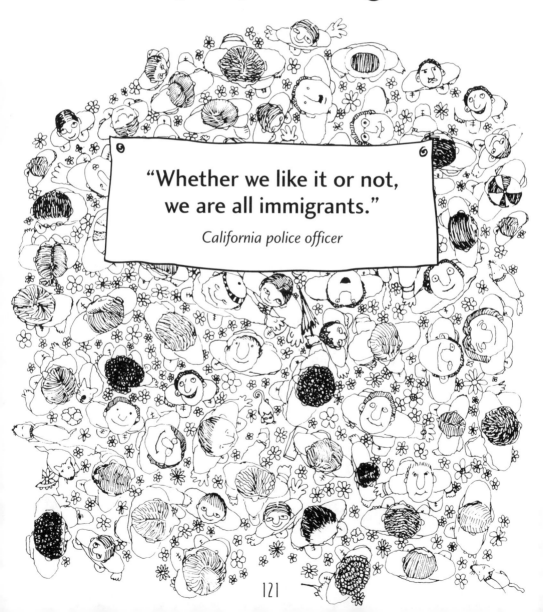

"Whether we like it or not,
we are all immigrants."

California police officer

Fight or flight

Diversity is exciting, but it causes problems, too. Or, rather, prejudice causes problems, and ignorance about diversity some-times intensifies prejudice.

The ethnic makeup of America is changing faster than ever, even faster than during the "immigration boom" of 1907, when nearly 12,000 people passed through Ellis Island in a single day. In other words, our world is changing faster than we can adapt, a situation that can trigger anxiety, frustration, and confusion. Put those three things together, and they often add up to insecurity, which can undermine your self-esteem and make you think that other people are the enemy or "it's all their fault."

Rapid change stimulates our "fight or flight response," developed tens of thousands of years ago when our ancestors lived in caves surrounded by wild animals. Back then, when a predator was nearby, the appropriate reaction was to try to escape, try to kill it, or risk being dinner for a saber-toothed tiger. Even though we're not in mortal danger every minute of the day anymore, we still react with anxiety, fear, and aggression to situations we perceive as threatening. The threat may be an ugly argument with someone about a touchy subject, a scary movie, or a belief that "they" are taking over.

A modern example of the "flight" response began during the 1970s, when white families started moving from the cities to the suburbs as black families moved into their urban neighborhoods. Whites believed that the presence of families of color would reduce the value of their homes and the quality of education in the city schools. This "white flight" is still going on today in neighborhoods across the country.

Hard times, hard feelings

In addition to the stress of fast-paced cultural change, when the economy isn't stable, people may lose their jobs and have a hard time finding new ones. Rents may rise or people may be forced to take pay cuts and look for cheaper housing, which is scarce in many places. Already underfunded social services—low-cost medical clinics, job training services—can't meet the needs of growing numbers of low-income families.

Then, when people read newspaper stories and watch TV news reports about the hundreds of thousands of immigrants—both legal and illegal—who are coming into the United States, many identify "them" as the problem. "Immigrants are bad," they reason, because they "take away" jobs, housing, educational opportunities, and other necessities from "real Americans." There are people who mistakenly believe that each Asian family that comes to the U.S. is given a free new car by the U.S. government.

TIME OUT

What do you think the term "real Americans" means? Have you heard anybody use it lately? In what context? Are immigrants "real Americans"? Why or why not? If not, what would make them "real Americans"?

● ● ● ● ● ● ● ● ● ● ● ●

Myths, misconceptions, and controversy

Some people believe that most immigrants are lazy. But many adult education classes are filled with Vietnamese, Tibetan, Hmong, Salvadoran, and Nicaraguan refugees, among others, who are working and studying hard to become more productive members of American society. Many didn't leave their countries by choice but were forced to flee violence and starvation. Since immigrants applying for citizenship have to pass a rigorous American history test, many may know more about our nation than most Americans.

The apple you had with lunch, the lettuce on your BLT, the sugar in your favorite soft drink, the wine your parents may drink, and countless other foods and beverages would never make it to your lunch tray, lunch bag, or dinner table if immigrants weren't willing to work for minimum wage. Many Americans, even uneducated and unskilled, refuse to accept poverty-level wages.

Some people believe that most immigrants go on welfare. In fact, studies suggest that immigrants contribute more in income tax, sales tax, and social security taxes than they get back in social services.

Immigrants have always been important to the United States, but their rapidly increasing numbers have sparked passionate controversy in recent years. In the early 1990s, a *New York Times*–CBS News poll showed that 61 percent of Americans believe that the United States admits too many immigrants.

According to Dan Stein, founder of the Federation for Immigration Reform, from 300,000 to one million immigrants enter the U.S. annually, "more than the population of Chicago, more than the population of the entire state of Arkansas." Stein thinks that our notions about immigration are out of date. Many Americans once felt that we were so prosperous compared to people in other countries that it was our duty to share the wealth. But today, Stein believes, we need to adopt a more practical attitude, taking care of the people who already live here before opening our doors to others. "Sure, Einstein was an immigrant," he admits. "But not every immigrant is Einstein."

Orange County, California, near the U.S.–Mexico border, spends $200 million a year on social services for immigrants, including medical care and job placement, and has recently proposed a three-year nationwide moratorium on all immigration. Immigration agents at John F. Kennedy Airport in New York stop 15,000 illegal aliens a year from entering the United States but have the capacity to detain only about 400. The others are released with instructions to appear later at a hearing, but few show up at their hearings.

Many aliens have no passports or other documents and immediately request political asylum whether or not they're eligible. Political asylum is granted to people whose lives are in danger from their governments.

TWO "SOLUTIONS"

In 1993, a weekly news program focused on Los Angeles. Some guests made recommendations for dealing with the immigration-related overcrowding and overspending that's a special problem in southern California.

■ Richard Rodriguez, Mexican American author and activist, suggested that after three generations in America, immigrants move back to their native countries.

■ Kathleen Brown, California state treasurer, suggested sending illegal aliens convicted of felonies back to their native countries. She explained that this could save California $500 million a year.

What do you think of these ideas?

P.S. Here are some interesting facts about that one-hour program:

■ Although it was taped in America's most multicultural city, only one person of color (Rodriguez) was interviewed at length.

■ The other commentators were four white males and two white females. Before the commentary portion of the program, one white female reporter and one white male reporter interviewed seven white males, three white females, one black male, and one Asian American female.

Quotas and restrictions

The United States has had official immigration quotas since 1921, when newcomers were limited to 358,000 per year. In the beginning, quotas changed with the country's needs. For instance, when the railroads were being built on the West Coast, large numbers of Chinese men were encouraged and sometimes coerced or paid to come to America, where they often lived in squalor, performed backbreaking labor for meager wages, and were not allowed to bring their wives and children. At other times, professionals like doctors, scientists, and college professors have been given preference. Sometimes people with unpopular political views have been refused entry.

Today some 600,000 legal immigrants enter the U.S. each year. There are people in Mexico and the Philippines who have been waiting for more than ten years to join their families in the United States.

In the late 1800s, immigrants who wanted to enter the United States had to be free of contagious diseases and mentally sound. They had to have friends or family already in the U.S., a place to stay, a profession, and a certain amount of money. Sometimes several poor families would pool their modest sums of money, and each in turn would show the combined cash to the customs inspectors as proof that they could support themselves. That's how much people wanted to live in the "Promised Land," the "Land of Plenty," and the "Gold Mountain," as immigrants called the United States.

There are still restrictions on who may enter the United States. Laws prevent more than 20,000 people from any one country from being given permanent resident visas annually. People from all over the world are still desperate to get in. Some pay as much as $25,000 or more for fake passports, other papers, and passage to the U.S. Many refugees die trying to get to America. In June, 1993, eight of 300 Chinese citizens seeking asylum in the U.S. drowned in icy New York Harbor when the freighter transporting them ran aground.

TIME OUT

How do you think the U.S. government should set immigration quotas? What should it do about illegal aliens? Should there be restrictions on who is and isn't allowed into the country? What kinds of restrictions?

Do you believe, like some people, that the U.S. has enough "foreigners" and we shouldn't admit more while millions of Americans are jobless, homeless, hungry, and without health insurance? Or do you believe, like other people, that it's our duty as a wealthy, democratic nation to share our resources with whoever needs them, no matter how much strain this puts on our economy?

Should we continue to honor the invitation in the famous poem by Emma Lazarus on the Statue of Liberty: *"Give me your tired, your poor, your huddled masses, yearning to be free"*?

● ● ● ● ● ● ● ● ● ● ●

What's your opinion?

If you're like most people, your opinions about immigration probably fall somewhere in between the two extremes. Maybe you need more information before you can take a stand.

Why not make this a special project? Consider one of these possibilities:

1. *Go to your library and find out as much as you can about immigration, past and present.* Read recent magazine articles on immigration. Talk to immigrants—people in your school, their parents, people in your neighborhood—and get their side of the story.

2.   *Put together a book, including photographs and biographies, of immigrants who have contributed to American culture and society.* Check with your librarian for ideas to get you started.

3.   *Choose a specific immigration-related issue to study.* Examples: the anti-immigration movement, the abuse of illegal aliens by their employers.

4.   *Arrange a school debate on the topic of immigration.* You might organize it around one of the questions in the Time Out on page 127.

5.   *Write a story about immigration for your school newspaper.* Or write a profile of a student at your school whose family immigrated to the United States. Or, if you're an immigrant, profile yourself. Tell how it felt to leave your country and come to the United States. Describe your experience, including the good parts and the not-so-good parts.

6.   *Even if you haven't formed an opinion about immigration, you can still call attention to immigration issues.* Write a letter to the editor of your city's daily newspaper, or volunteer to do a public service announcement for a local television station.

Scapegoating: An easy way out

Take rapid, dramatic cultural changes, add economic strain, throw in ignorance of other cultures and lack of meaningful contact (such as working together or worshipping together) with people who are different, and you get intergroup conflict—in schools, neighborhoods, and cities.

Intergroup conflict means what it sounds like: conflict between two or more groups of people. It may include anything from harsh words and resentments to cross burnings, racist graffiti, and violence. But whatever the end result may be, it often begins with scapegoating.

Think of a time when you were blamed for something you didn't do, or a time when you were punished because somebody was having a bad day, and you'll understand how it feels to be a scapegoat. Even if it happened a long time ago, chances are it still hurts or makes you angry to remember it.

Scapegoating isn't right and it isn't fair—not for the interracial couple who finds a flaming cross in their yard at three o'clock in the morning, not for the Asian student whose classmates taunt "Chop chop, so solly" whenever they see him, not for the homosexuals who get beaten up and called "faggots" and "dykes."

During the Persian Gulf War, attacks on Arab Americans increased significantly, even though many of the victims weren't of Arab descent. They just "looked like Arabs."

African Americans, Arab Americans, Asian Americans, and many other groups are paying the price for the fear many Americans feel—fear of losing their jobs, their self-respect, the American Dream. That fear leads to a desire to blame someone else. Blaming is easier than trying to understand what's really causing the problems and doing the hard work needed to solve them.

"So the moral decay in our society gets blamed on gay men and lesbians," observes longtime Seattle human rights worker Bill Wassmuth. "The job loss gets blamed on Hispanics and African Americans. And the economic problems get blamed on the Jews."

Being different can be dangerous

Some people don't differentiate between newly arrived immigrants and second- or third-generation immigrants. Instead, they see all people with "foreign" ancestry or dark skin as "the enemy" —including African Americans, who have been an integral part of our nation for hundreds of years. Being the constant targets of hatred and fear strips people of their individuality and dignity. They are seen as symbols of what's wrong with society, as "less human" than whites.

Some psychologists believe that the feeling that some people are "more human" than others was in part responsible for the Holocaust. The Nazis murdered millions of Jews, homosexuals, handicapped people, Jehovah's Witnesses, and gypsies—anyone who didn't fit the Nazis' image of the "ideal human."

After participating in a Building Bridges race relations workshop in Memphis, Tennessee, a high school student named Garland said that she had never considered herself prejudiced before. "I guess I really didn't think blacks were people," she admitted. "I don't know what I was thinking."

1. Do you know of any situations in the world today in which groups of people are treated as inferior, the way the Nazis treated Jews, homosexuals, disabled people, and others they considered less deserving of life than the people they favored?

2. If you said "no," what about the "ethnic cleansing" in Bosnia?

3. Can you think of three examples to support the statement, "Being different can be dangerous"?

4. What do you think Garland, the Memphis student, meant when she said, "I guess I really didn't think blacks were people"?

Getting along in a changing world...

Project 10: Helping Students Accept Sexual Differences

"I no longer consider myself stigmatized
or different from other students."

Gregory

"Dear Mom," read the note on the refrigerator. "I'm a homosexual. I'll be home around 10 tonight. Love, Keith."

Keith's note may make you smile because he's trying so hard to be casual about something so important. But telling his parents he's gay is probably one of the hardest things Keith has ever done in his life. Let's hope his parents love him enough to accept him just the way he is. Like the mother who wrote in the *New York Times*: "My daughter is a lesbian. She also is the light of my life, a warm and talented young woman whose joyous spirit helps brighten the lives of others."

If Keith's parents are not that supportive, hopefully he has access to an organization like Project 10. Founded in 1984 at Fairfax High School in Los Angeles by teacher-counselor Virginia

Uribe, Project 10 is a dropout prevention-education-counseling program targeting gay and lesbian students. It also benefits heterosexual students by challenging their stereotypes about their homosexual classmates and helping them learn to accept all kinds of differences—sexual, racial, and religious.

Counselors help gay and lesbian students deal with the low self-esteem and feelings of isolation and alienation that often plague young people who have a "different" sexual orientation. Gay and lesbian students support one another in group discussions when they talk about problems they encounter in school—problems like the incident that inspired Virginia Uribe to start Project 10 in the first place.

Chris was a 17-year-old homosexual who had been forced to live on the streets at age 14, when his parents learned he was gay. After that, he was hounded out of school after school because of his sexual orientation. As reported in the *Project 10 Handbook*, he was physically and verbally abused by his classmates—and harassed by some of his teachers—from his first day at Fairfax High. After a few weeks, Chris dropped out and went back "home" to the streets.

The goals of Project 10's adult and teenage counselors include suicide prevention; providing accurate information about AIDS; educating classmates, parents, teachers, and administrators about homosexuality; and offering substance abuse counseling. But their most important objective is to make sure that a note left on the refrigerator doesn't become a ticket to misery and self-loathing.

The people involved in the project hope that more gay and lesbian students will be able to relate to the graduate speech of a student named Gregory. He spoke of preparing to leave "a place where I feel so at peace with myself…. Being associated with Project 10 has given me the chance to articulate the needs of the silent majority…. I no longer consider myself stigmatized or different from other students…. From feelings of hopelessness when I came to Fairfax, I now feel good about myself and look forward to a happy and successful future."

Getting along in a changing world...

Homosexuals:
More than Sexuality

"The rain falls on every roof; the sun shines upon all alike."
African proverb

It's easy to get the impression from the news media that the main difference between homosexuals and heterosexuals is that sex is the main focus of life for gay men and lesbians. But just as there's much more to heterosexual life than physical intimacy, gay and lesbian life also includes dozens of other things: doing homework and household chores, watching TV, going to movies and concerts with friends, having your teeth cleaned, taking care of pets, wanting a bigger allowance, and pondering the mysteries of the universe, to name a few.

It also should include the right to live free of harassment. But homosexuals are frequent targets of hate crime, and hate crimes against gay men and lesbians tend to be more brutal than other hate crimes. As a result, gay men and lesbians have to change their behavior or risk being victimized.

Imagine not being able to hold hands in public with someone you care about without being called names, threatened, or attacked.

Imagine being asked to leave home because of your sexual orientation. (In the San Francisco Bay Area, 26 percent of the males living on the streets have been thrown out of their homes by their parents, according to *MediaFile,* a publication of the Media Alliance.)

Imagine not being able to be honest about yourself with friends and family because you're afraid they'll abandon you. But that doesn't always happen. Some family members, like 18-year-old John's mother, are more understanding than others. As John recalls, "I told my mother I was gay driving home from Los Angeles at Christmas vacation and she said, 'It's about time you told me.'"

Here are a few more things to keep in mind about homosexuality:

■ Don't assume that someone is gay or lesbian because he or she "looks" gay or lesbian. Ask yourself, "What does that mean, anyway? Where do I get my ideas about how homosexuals look?"

■ Don't assume that someone isn't gay or lesbian because he or she doesn't "look" it.

■ Just because you have warm feelings about a same-sex friend doesn't mean that you're gay or lesbian.

■ Just because a gay or lesbian friend has warm feelings about you doesn't mean that he or she wants or expects anything more than friendship.

■ Some people seem to think that all gay men and lesbians are attracted to all heterosexual men and women. Are all "straight" women attracted to all "straight" men, and vice versa?

■ Don't assume that someone who is gay or lesbian wants to "recruit" or "convert" others to homosexuality. Do you go around trying to convince homosexual classmates to "go straight"?

If you have questions about sexual orientation, talk to an adult you trust and feel comfortable with. If you can't find an adult to talk to, look in the yellow pages for a teen hotline, and discuss your concerns with a trained counselor.

CHAPTER 9

Updating Your Files

"We as individuals can just
make a little effort every day
to try and understand
one person that
we come across."

Texas twelfth grader

135

Mixed messages

Mixed messages, cultural misunderstandings, crossed signals—whatever you call them, they can lead to confusion, hurt feelings, and resentment. Unless you take time to learn about them *before* they happen.

Did you know that a friendly wave in one culture may be considered offensive or hostile in another? Or that some people perceive steady eye contact as a sign of paying attention, while others think it's rude and threatening? Some Asian merchants don't touch their customers' hands or make eye contact when taking money and giving change because those are intimate gestures to them. Customers who don't understand that this behavior is cultural rather than personal may feel insulted or angry. To Americans, solemn-looking Asians may seem unapproachable, while Asians sometimes observe that Americans smile so much that they look foolish.

By the way, don't feel insulted if a Tibetan sticks her tongue out at you. It just means "hi." In some parts of New Guinea, males pat each others' buttocks in greeting.

Being aware of these differences not only makes communication easier, it also keeps people from forming the stereotypes that lead to prejudice and racism.

Invisible "isms"

It's a normal human tendency to stereotype people and places. That's one way we put together our mental picture of the world and how it works, the map that guides our daily actions. But sometimes we forget to change the map, even when we discover that some of the roads are closed, dead ends have been extended to meet other roads, and new bridges have been built.

Have you ever heard anybody say that people who live in Los Angeles all have car phones and swimming pools? That New Yorkers are obnoxious? That people who live in Nashville all like

country music? Although there may be some truth to those gener-
alizations—some Los Angelenos have car phones and pools, some
New Yorkers are obnoxious, some Nashville residents like country
music—they're tiny fragments of much larger, more complex
truths. In short, they are stereotypes.

We even have stereotypes about racism. If you don't believe it,
write down the first three things and/or people that come to mind
when you think about racist behavior. Is Adolf Hitler on your list?
How about neo-Nazi skinhead gangs? Burning crosses and white
hoods? Swastikas and Confederate flags? Actually, racism is seldom
that obvious, and racists often turn out to be "average citizens"
rather than extremists—your piano teacher, a family next door,
your best friend's brother, even members of your own family.

Sometimes racism is invisible, even to the racist. That's
because it can be unconscious, hidden deep inside our minds. How
does it get there? When we hear stereotypes and prejudicial statements often enough, we begin to believe them…even when they're
about us.

How would you respond if someone accused you of being a
racist, or prejudiced against certain groups of people? If you like to
believe that you're fair-minded, you probably would deny the accu-
sation. You might even feel insulted, hurt, or angry. Most people
don't want to be associated with groups who celebrate Hitler's
birthday, hold "white power" rallies, and publicly declare their
hatred for people of color, Jews, and homosexuals.

So, you're not prejudiced? Read these statements, then decide
if they are true or false. Don't think about them; just give the first
answer that comes to mind:

1.   People who are obese don't have any willpower.

2.   AIDS is a gay disease.

3.   Poor Hispanic people are all on welfare.

4.   All young black men are gang members, drug dealers, thieves,
or all three.

The answers? All are false. Dieting, which requires consider-
able willpower, can actually cause or perpetuate obesity. Many

heterosexual people have contracted (and spread) the AIDS virus. Statistics show that most welfare recipients are white, not people of color. And here's how it feels to be a black man who's falsely perceived as a criminal by people who don't even know him: "It hurts when people move away from me on the subway because I'm black, and some black guys rob people…. It gets to you after awhile…. I've never robbed anybody in my life. It's not my nature."

"ISMS" THAT AFFECT OUR LIVES

by Shane Jenner, age 11
Webster Open School
Minneapolis, Minnesota

"Isms" aren't something you can go to the doctor for, but they sure can make you sick. This year at Webster Open School we have been studying the "isms."

RACISM

It tears people apart, it separates them because of their color and limits who can be your friends.

SEXISM

It divides people into groups of boys and girls and makes them stay there. At the beginning of this trimester, I noticed something that made me sick, but I couldn't go to the doctor for it. One class seated itself with boys on one side and girls on the other. I noticed because I was the only boy on the girls' side! After all, people should be able to be friends with both genders!

CLASSISM

Classism discriminates against people because of money. It's sad when *things* are so important they come before people. Things don't make good friends.

You may think there is no cure for the "isms," but you just have to fight them. Fighting them doesn't mean "putting up your dukes." It means learning about the "isms."

From *Generator*, the National Youth Leadership Conference newsletter, Spring 1993. Used with permission.

Listening to your self-talk

How can you find out if you have invisible "isms"? Start by listening to your self-talk—the things you tell yourself inside your head. You'll have to pay attention, because self-talk is so automatic— we "whisper" it so softly—that it's hard to catch ourselves doing it.

Some self-talk is positive. It keeps us safe ("Look both ways before crossing the street"). It helps us to feel good about ourselves ("I can do it"). It motivates us to try things we might not do other- wise ("Go ahead…call her! Just pick up the phone and dial!"). It reminds us of things that need doing ("Math test tomorrow…don't forget to study").

But other self-talk is negative, and here is where you can usually find your invisible "isms."

Do you use "all," "always," and "never" when you think about certain groups of people? As in "All rock stars use drugs," "Arabs always try to cheat you," or "Blacks never make good managers?" That's prejudice talking.

Have you ever thought anything like "I can't believe Jenny hangs out with that Iranian girl. She's so strange-looking"? If you catch yourself in this kind of self-talk, try "talking back": "Just because Nabella has darker skin doesn't mean she's 'strange-looking.'"

Your prejudiced self-talk doesn't necessarily have to be your own voice. It could be something you've heard a friend or neighbor say, some stereotype you've seen a thousand times on television, something you've come to believe even though it isn't true.

Here's another sign of prejudiced self-talk: You find yourself thinking of a person in terms of a racial or cultural group rather than as an individual. For instance, if Rachael is "my Jewish friend" instead of "my friend who loves scary movies," or if Mark is "a crippled neighbor" and not "my next-door neighbor" or "the neighbor who has the dachshund," or if Robert is "a black guy" and Elliott is just "a guy" (meaning "a white guy"), you're self-talking in stereotypes.

Another kind of thinking to watch out for is "blaming the victim." For instance: "If she hadn't been out so late, she wouldn't have been raped." Or: "He should have known better than to date a white girl." Blaming the victim makes it easier to deny your own prejudices.

"They're all alike"

When we stereotype people, we focus on assumed characteristics, often perceived as negative. For instance: "Men who cry are weak." "Asians are overachievers." "Blacks all smoke crack cocaine."

Stereotyping plays a crucial role in prejudice, racism, discrimination and hate crime—crime motivated by an individual's hatred for someone of another race, religion, gender, ethnicity, or sexual orientation. In fact, without stereotypes, prejudice, racism, and discrimination wouldn't exist. "You can't judge a book by its cover," goes the old saying. But that's exactly what we do, even though we know better, when we're confronted by people who aren't like us.

We would never label a container without looking inside first, but when it comes to people, we take one look and decide we know a lot about them. A rich person is "spoiled and lazy," a thin person is "vain," someone with red hair is "hot-tempered," a blonde is "dumb" or "stuck-up." From there, we assume that *all* people in each group (rich, thin, red-haired, blonde) have these same negative characteristics.

Judging the outside without knowing the inside; lumping individuals together into groups because they share a single characteristic; forming an opinion about a group based on the behavior of a few people ("all politicians are dishonest")—these are what stereotyping involves.

CAST FROM THE SAME MOLD

The original meaning of the word "stereotype" is "a plate cast from a printing surface." Type for printing books, posters, etc. used to be "composed," or set, by hand. A mold was made from the composed type, and the mold was then used to make a metal printing plate— a stereotype. Many identical plates could be made. Can you see the connection between the original meaning and the way we use this word today?

Updating your files

Stereotypes and prejudices are like old computer programs inside our heads or a file cabinet we haven't cleaned out in years. They operate so automatically we aren't even aware they're there. But you can learn to notice them—and change them.

Sometimes the information we've saved in computer files or file folders—labeled "Women," "Fat People," "Old People," "White People," "Catholics," etc.—is out of date or was wrong to begin with. But our brains keep going to those files whenever we need information about those groups of people.

TIME OUT

Get some envelopes and label each one with the name of a group— "Doctors," "Truck Drivers," "Jews," "Anti-Abortion Advocates," whatever.

141

List five things you believe about each group and put your list inside the envelope.

Read your lists carefully. Where did you get your information? How long ago? Cross out anything you think may be out of date or wrong. Replace it with a nonjudgmental observation. Make a note and add it to the envelope whenever you see or learn something that doesn't fit your preconceived ideas.

For instance, instead of "Doctors make too much money," how about "Doctors deserve to be paid well for the long hours they work"? Instead of "Truck drivers are rude," how about "Truck drivers are under a lot of pressure to meet delivery schedules"? Instead of "Jews have weird holidays," how about "Jews celebrate Hanukkah around the same time Christians celebrate Christmas"? Instead of "Anti-abortion advocates are right-wing fanatics," how about "Anti-abortion advocates have strong feelings about abortion that sometimes lead to confrontation"?

● ● ● ● ● ● ● ● ● ● ● ●

Changing channels

Another way to think of your brain is as a television receiver. Maybe it's an old-fashioned TV with an antenna on the roof, and it only picks up a few channels in your immediate area, so the information it brings in is limited. On the other hand, if you have cable, you have access to dozens of regional channels and a few "superstations" that broadcast over long distances.

Now imagine that the signals you receive represent knowledge about different people and cultures. Obviously you can learn more if you have cable. In fact, the best kind of brain for understanding diversity would be one with a satellite dish, capable of picking up stations from around the world. The more stations you have, the more you can learn.

How can you develop a "satellite dish" brain? Keep reading.

Six ways to expand your world

1. *Get to know someone who isn't like you.* This might be a person of a different culture, race, religion, or sexual orientation; someone older or younger than you; someone with epilepsy, cerebral palsy, or Down syndrome.

Getting to know new people can be tough, so start simple, maybe with a classmate who belongs to a religion you don't know much about. Ask if you can go to church, temple, or meeting with him or her. Later, ask your friend to explain the rituals and other events you observed during the service.

2. *See if your new friend will invite you to share a cultural holiday.* Some possibilities:

- Kwaanza, a seven-day African American heritage celebration based on African harvest festivals

- Chinese New Year, a traditional spring festival featuring dragons, fireworks, and parades

- Divali, the Hindu festival of lights

- St. Patrick's Day, an Irish festival in honor of a popular saint

- Cinco de Mayo, a Mexican celebration

- A Native American gourd dance or round dance.

3. *Eat lunch with somebody new at least once a month.* Promise yourself that, by the end of the year, you'll get to know three people (or more) outside your regular group of friends.

Before you first meet someone, write in a journal any preconceived ideas about him or her and what you think triggered your ideas. After a few months, go back and read what you wrote. Have your ideas changed? Update your files.

4. *Look for common ground.* Spend at least ten minutes each week talking to someone you think is not at all like you. Try to find something you have in common—an idea, a belief, an interest. You'll find that most people have at least a few things in common, even if they seem completely different at first.

5.   *Ask new people you meet to do something with you.* A young girl who has dozens of friends does this with almost everyone she meets. She invites them to a movie or some other activity. A lot of them, she says, become good friends.

6.   *Volunteer to read to or visit with an older person in your neighborhood or in a nursing home.* Do this on a regular basis—once a month, or once a week. Ask the person to tell you about his or her life. Make a certificate honoring something brave or remarkable the person has done, sign it, and present it to him or her. Everyone has done lots of brave and remarkable things by the time they're over 60.

1.   How many stereotypes about yourself can you think of? Do you believe any of them?

2.   Think of at least three senior citizens you know (or know about) who are role models. For instance, I know an 80-year-old graduate student who spent three years in Botswana, Africa, as a Peace Corps volunteer when she was in her 60s, and she learned to fly at age 60.

3.   Write down your own personal strategy for fighting the "isms" Shane Jenner describes in his essay.

New Moon Magazine: Questioning Gender Bias and Celebrating Young Womanhood

"I don't think Barbie should go around saying math is tough."

Anna Geronimas

"When you finish college, why do you get a Bachelor's degree?"
"Why can't Minnie Mouse wear a baseball cap instead of a bow?"
"Why is a king higher than a queen in cards?"
These are just three of the many questions asked by writers and readers of *New Moon: The Magazine for Girls and Their Dreams*, a bimonthly publication created to inspire and empower girls and give them the courage to stick up for themselves in the face of discrimination. The colorful, upbeat magazine is fun to read, too.

Most magazines for women—teenagers and adults—focus on dieting, dating, makeup, and clothes. But the young women who work on *New Moon* write about "real girls"—girls like themselves who would rather read an interview with the first woman to reach the North Pole than with the first supermodel to pose at the North Pole.

SHERRY BOYCE

The New Moon editorial board at work

New Moon explores the differences between what society expects of girls and boys and stresses being yourself and valuing achievements over appearance and material possessions. Readers contribute stories, poems, folk tales, cartoons, artwork, diary excerpts, and reviews for books, movies, music, and software programs. In a column called "How Aggravating," readers write about unfair stuff that drives them crazy, like a Barbie doll that says, "Math is tough." (As a result of parents' and kids' complaints, that Barbie was taken off the market.)

Each issue of *New Moon* contains "herstory" calendars focusing on women's achievements and fun facts about women. (Did you know that the month of June was named for Juno, queen of the ancient Roman deities?) "The Global Village" is a regular column describing "a girl's life somewhere in the world." One issue featured Iceland and included information about Icelandic naming customs, instructions for making an Icelandic family tree, and a page of vital statistics about the country, decorated with drawings of walruses and penguins playing on icebergs.

Other articles are about current events, body language, and exceptional women—like explorer Ann Bancroft, the first woman to reach the North Pole, and Sor Juana Ines de la Cruz, a 17th-century Mexican poet. There are articles about customs from different countries, and instructions for making things—a compass and a stargazer, for instance. And there are plenty of cartoons, riddles, and knock-knock jokes.

The 25-member *New Moon* editorial board ranges in age from eight to 14 years old, and their work has earned the magazine 5,000 subscribers, quite a few of whom live in other countries. Co-publishers Joe Kelly and his wife, Nancy Gruver, offer guidance and help with the desktop publishing software used to produce *New Moon*. But the ideas and creative decisions come from the editorial board and the readers.

Here's what some of them have to say about *New Moon:*

- "It is the first magazine that is actually for girls. It is also what girls actually think."

- "It's fun. I get to know a lot of stuff I would not get to know otherwise. I also get some input, which I like *very much*."

For more information about *New Moon*, write or call:

New Moon Publishers
P.O. Box 3587
Duluth, MN 55803
Telephone: (218) 728-5507

CHAPTER 10

Hate Groups

"Whatever their faults,
they tell themselves,
at least they're white."

*Michael Kronenwetter,
author of* United They Hate

United by prejudice

By reading this book, you're showing that you're willing to keep an open mind about differences. If you have prejudices, you're willing to take another look at them and maybe change your mind. But what about young people who already have learned to mistrust, fear, or hate anyone different from them? What happens to them as our global culture becomes more diverse?

Some "outgrow" their prejudices as positive experiences with people of different races, religions, and ethnicities replace their preconceived ideas. Many continue to feel resentment and hostility toward people of different races, religions, and ethnic groups, no matter what. These are the people who tell AIDS jokes, refuse to vote for "minorities," and call feminists "feminazis." But they rarely express their feelings in public or violent ways.

Others join hate groups—individuals united by prejudice against people of other races, ethnic origins, religions, or sexual orientations. They seek out the company of others who share their fears and hostilities, and act them out by harassing and assaulting their "enemies."

That's what Ben did. Being part of a racist skinhead group made the 14-year-old Canadian feel powerful and gave him a purpose—a cause. He felt like a nationalist warrior, fighting for his country and protecting it from "outsiders"—immigrants.

In multiracial, multicultural Toronto, there are tens of thousands of "outsiders." More than 50 percent of the city's students come from families who speak neither English nor French. From a racist skinhead's point of view, this is proof that "they" are taking over, a common fear among racists.

Why do some kids become skinheads?

Like all young people, those who become skinheads need a sense of belonging, a feeling that they "fit" somewhere. They need to be accepted by a group of their peers.

Skinheads often have failed to earn acceptance in traditional ways. They may have tried out for athletic teams, hoped to pledge fraternities or sororities, auditioned for parts in school plays, or applied for positions on school papers and yearbooks. When they didn't make the team, the grade, the play, or the paper—and especially when people of different races did—they sought honors and acceptance elsewhere.

Ben's "badges" were the words "SKIN" tattooed on his shoulder blade and "EAST END BOYS" tattooed on his forearm. As a member of the East End Boys, Ben felt that he had become part of a worldwide movement of white working-class youth who were proud of their racial heritage and united against the "anti-white system."

WHO ARE THE RACISTS?

Racism isn't restricted to the so-called "working classes" or to one race. People from all races and segments of society feel bitterness toward one another and support the activities of racist groups, even though they may not personally take action or commit hate crimes. It's estimated that for every Klan member and racist skinhead, there may be as many as ten sympathizers and supporters.

And racism isn't always directed at minorities. Members of the majority culture (white heterosexuals) can be targets, too. One of the plays Hoffman Estates High School students performed during their awareness-raising program (see pages 20–21) described a Puerto Rican family's distress about their daughter dating a white classmate. And hate crimes against whites have increased considerably over the past few years.

What do skinheads believe?

Some young people become skinheads because they feel that this gives them permission to express their rage and frustration through violence. As one skinhead leader proclaimed, "I am a violent person. I love the white race, and if you love something, you're the most vicious person on earth."

Skinheads believe that violence is an acceptable way to solve problems and relieve frustration. Nicknames like "Batman" and "Death" are well-earned. In Portland, Oregon, skinheads used a baseball bat to club an Ethiopian man to death. In New York City, skinheads lured a gay man to a dark, deserted school yard, then beat him to death with a hammer. In Port Arthur, Texas, skinheads were charged with killing a man as part of a gang initiation. Skinheads even kill each other—to avenge real or imagined insults or to establish dominance. They may steal each others' jackets or boots (their most prized possessions), a practice they call "taxing." They rarely plan their attacks. They prefer to work in groups, which boosts their courage, even when attacking a single victim.

Other skinhead crimes include spray-painting swastikas and white power slogans on synagogues; spray-painting or otherwise vandalizing businesses and homes owned by Jews, blacks, gays, and immigrants; and yelling racial or sexual slurs. They also enjoy marching with swastika shields and banners, chanting racist battle cries, and flashing stiff-armed Nazi salutes.

The Final Solution

Ben belonged to this violent subculture for four years—until he took a course called "Facing History and Ourselves." The course was designed to educate students about the Holocaust, the slaughter of millions of Jews, people with handicaps, gypsies, Jehovah's Witnesses, homosexuals, political dissidents, and other "inferior" people during World War II.

Hitler and his followers believed that light-skinned, blue-eyed men and women were genetically superior to all others. By destroying inferior "specimens," Hitler believed that he could create a master race of supermen and superwomen and, with their help, conquer the world. His anti-Semitic propaganda was passed into law, and concentration camps were set up as killing factories for the people he despised.

Hitler's plan was known as the Final Solution, a name recently borrowed by a white power rock band. Many Holocaust scholars believe that a gradual decline in tolerance and the belief that some people deserved to live more than others were responsible for the widespread acceptance of the Nazis' hideous war crimes.

Do you think those things exist today? Do you think another Holocaust could happen?

A GRADUAL DECLINE IN TOLERANCE TODAY

Consider these incidents reported by Klanwatch, a project of the Southern Poverty Law Center:

■ In 1993, Oregon residents voted against a proposal that would guarantee civil rights to homosexuals. Those voters believe that homosexuals are already protected by the Constitution, and the proposed law amounts to "special treatment" for gay men and lesbians. (In Colorado, where a similar proposal was defeated, the state supreme court struck down the vote as unconstitutional.)

■ In 1992, American Girl Scouts with Asian features selling cookies in front of a Ventura, California, supermarket were called "Japs" and told "I only buy American" by passing adults.

■ In 1993 in Tampa, Florida, two white men put a rope around a black coworker's neck and burned a small cross in front of him.

■ In 1993, an anti-Semitic note was placed in a Jewish student's locker in a Mount Olive, New Jersey, school.

■ A group of young blacks attacked some whites after a Dallas Cowboys parade in 1993.

■ Most organizations that monitor hate crime, including the Anti-Defamation League, the Center for Democratic Renewal, and

Klanwatch, report a steady increase in hate crime over the past several years.

- Statistics show that most hate crimes are committed by people younger than 19 years of age.

Many organizations report that intolerance has never been more likely to erupt into violence than it is today, not even during the racial turmoil of the 1960s Civil Rights Movement.

Some experts believe that the rise in hate crime may be due partly to better public education about hate crime, which leads to more people reporting the crimes. On the other hand, Danny Welch, director of Klanwatch, which monitors hate group activities, believes that "more than half of all hate crimes are never reported to police," and many of those that are reported are not recorded as hate crimes. Welch adds that most hate crimes committed on school grounds and college campuses are not reported.

A skinhead faces his fears

The more Ben learned about Hitler and the Holocaust from "Facing History and Ourselves," the more he questioned his own racist, nationalist, anti-immigrant, anti-Semitic beliefs. Eventually, this self-examination changed his life. He let his hair grow, traded his combat boots for running shoes, and started working with Justice for Children, an organization that helps young criminals.

"The most difficult part of 'Facing History' was looking at myself and realizing how easy it is for people to be manipulated to do the wrong thing," Ben now says. He believes that the course should be required for all students.

Kids in the Klan

She looks four or five years old, scowling at the camera like any other child who doesn't want to stand still long enough to have her picture taken. But, other than that, she's like something out of a nightmare. Barely old enough to read, she should be dressed in jeans and carrying a stuffed animal. Instead, she's wearing child-sized Ku Klux Klan robes and holding a nightstick, a club used by police to maintain order in potentially violent situations.

Is she just playing dress-up with her parents? Or does she already believe, as they do, that the white race is superior to all others? Does she believe, like her parents, that blacks should be sent back to Africa, homosexuals should be executed, and Jews, Asians, and Hispanics are subhuman?

Since children learn by example, the answer to the last two questions is probably yes. Without knowing why, she already hates blacks, Jews, gay men, lesbians, immigrants, and anyone else not like her and her family. What might be a frown of annoyance could just as easily be the face of hatred.

Her picture appeared in *The Ku Klux Klan: A History of Racism and Violence,* a special report produced by Klanwatch. It was taken at least ten years ago. By now, as a teenager or a young adult, she may be a full-fledged, active member of America's oldest hate group. Or maybe, like Ben, she had an experience that led her to question the group's hate-filled philosophy and changed her life.

RACISM ON-LINE

The white supremacist group Aryan Nations runs a computer bulletin board system (BBS). Called "Liberty Net," it allows users throughout the United States to read racist propaganda and swap racist jokes. The BBS also gives instructions for making homemade weapons and highlights upcoming white supremacist gatherings. Periodically, it invites users to enter names, addresses, and telephone number of "queers" for upcoming "round-ups."

Night rides and slave patrols

The Klan was formed after the Civil War to terrorize former slaves and keep them from taking advantage of their new freedom. Since the Confederacy had fought to preserve slavery, Klan members wore hooded robes to conceal their faces and make their victims think they were the ghosts of dead Confederate soldiers.

Klansmen used "night rides," lynchings, and whippings to control former slaves and intimidate white people who sympathized with them. In *Night Riders in Black Folk History*, author Gladys-Marie Fry explains that the night rides imitated earlier "slave patrols." A story from her book, passed down from slaves after the Civil War, tells how plantation owners made sure their servants and field hands stayed on the plantation and out of trouble at night: "Most every night along about eight or nine o'clock, this overseer would get on his white horse and put a sheet over him, and put tin cans on a rope and drag it around. And they told the slaves, 'Now if you poke your head outdoors after a certain time, a monster of a ghost will get you.'" These threats almost always worked, so it's no surprise that the Klan chose similar costumes and methods.

In later years, the Klan (which consists today of at least two dozen separate factions, or groups) added Jews, Catholics, and immigrants to its hate list. Anti-Catholic sentiments may be softening; one of the Klan's Imperial Wizards (national leaders) was a Catholic.

How the Klan sees itself

■ In October of 1991, Douglas M. Garner, a member of the North Carolina Invisible Empire Knights of the Ku Klux Klan, pleaded guilty to possessing a homemade bomb which he planned to use to intimidate a black man involved in an interracial relationship.

■ In May of 1991, Louisiana Invisible Empire members carried out a series of cross burnings meant to frighten minorities. Their actions were orchestrated from prison by Wayne Pierce.

■ In 1992, Joseph Doak, New Jersey Invisible Empire state leader, and Harold Patterson, his security guard, were convicted of plotting to murder two rival Klansmen in 1990.

Those are just a few of the incidents connected to a single Klan faction. Yet today's Klan denies its history of violence. It claims to be "pro-white" rather than anti-black and anti-Semitic. But a look at the pamphlets and newsletters passed out at rallies and mailed to members paints a different picture.

One newsletter, "The White Patriot," claims that "the Klan believes in LOVE." Anti-Klan forces, it insists, are the *real* haters. The same newsletter glorifies motherhood while attacking the supporters of women's rights. It offers for sale anti-Semitic publications with titles like "The Jewish Conspiracy," which presents "proof" that Jews control the government and the media.

"The White Patriot" also accuses the media of promoting homosexuality, "race-mixing" (interracial marriage), and abortion. "We want the queers put back in the closet," declares an article called "KKK and the Media." "The only way to stop AIDS is to completely stop the free movement of queers in our society where they spread their infectious disease. We want the complete stop of illegal aliens that are now flooding across our border and which steal jobs and wealth of Americans."

The Klan goes to school

Today's Klan factions, skinheads, and other white supremacist groups try to recruit new members from middle schools and high schools. The most common method is to move in wherever there's racial tension and offer the students help. For instance, in Covington, Georgia, when high school students protested the naming of two valedictorians—one black, one white—the Klan was nearby, passing out literature.

After fights between black and white students in St. Louis, Missouri, the Knights of the Ku Klux Klan posted fliers around the school proclaiming "Help Stop Black Crime!" They were illustrated with a drawing of a hooded man holding an automatic weapon.

The group's mailing address appeared under the slogan "Racial Purity is America's Security."

In situations like these, Klan members sometimes win new recruits by siding with students against authority figures like teachers and principals. To confused young people who may believe that adults don't understand them or respect their ideas, this can be very appealing. Also, belonging to an "outlaw" organization such as the Klan offers rebellious teenagers a way to assert their growing need for independence. Many teens, at least at first, don't realize how far outside the law Klan groups are willing to go to achieve their goals.

TIME OUT

What would you do if there was racial tension at your school and the Klan showed up? If you were approached by Klan members or skinheads? If someone tried to give you hate literature?

Ask your social studies teacher if you can spend a class or two exploring these questions. Form groups to create role plays and propose several solutions. Do the role plays and discuss them afterward.

Before you do the role plays, be sure to read "If we ignore them, won't they go away?" on pages 160–162.

● ● ● ● ● ● ● ● ● ● ● ●

Hate groups and self-esteem

Everyone needs to belong to a group of some kind, whether it's a family, a fraternity or sorority, a school club, a church, a gang, or a hate group. Membership helps us to form a sense of identity, a mental and emotional picture of who we are and where we fit into the world. This in turn gives us self-esteem, a solid foundation in an otherwise shaky world.

But why do some people join bands or environmental groups while others become skinheads and Klan members? Many, like the little girl pictured in the Klanwatch magazine, are following their parents' example. But a 1988 study conducted by Boise State University and the Idaho Human Rights Coalition found that some young adults are even *more* prejudiced than their parents, so "like father, like son" or "like mother, like daughter" isn't the whole story.

In fact, there is no simple answer to this question. But there are some characteristics shared by many young people (and adults) who join hate groups. These characteristics are also found in other young people who commit hate crimes without belonging to racist organizations.

One almost universal trait is the lack of self-esteem. One former skinhead described his fellow white supremacists as "so filled with hatred that they even hate themselves." For many, their acts of violence have little or nothing to do with their victims. Instead, they are expressions of rage and self-loathing.

According to Michael Kronenwetter, author of *United They Hate: White Supremacist Groups in America,* "Some believe membership will give them power, which in turn will bring self-confidence" and the respect of others. Kronenwetter adds that these alienated losers don't necessarily hate minorities. Instead, they accept the groups' racist philosophy because that's what they have to do to belong. Those who do believe in white superiority, he says, "need to feel their race is special so they can feel special. Whatever their faults, they tell themselves, at least they're white."

SKINHEAD STYLE

- Some skinheads are fans of "Oi!," a type of angry British working-class punk rock music. They practice "slam-dancing," a type of dancing in which people violently slam their bodies together.

- Some groups and individuals just adopt the skinhead style—close-cropped hair, steel-toed combat boots (used by violent skins to kick their victims), flight jackets, braces (suspenders), and tattoos—but not the skinhead philosophy. They use the look to attract attention, intimidate people, and express rebellion against conformity and authority. There are even weekend "wannabe" skins, who dress like skins on Fridays and Saturdays and turn back into ordinary teenagers during the week.

- Although most skinhead groups are violent, not all are racist or neo-Nazi. The skinhead acronym SHARP, for instance, stands for "Skinheads Against Racial Prejudice." SHARP members often engage in bloody confrontations with racist skins.

- Not all skinheads are white. There are black, Asian, and Hispanic skins, too.

If we ignore them, won't they go away?

The greatest allies a hate group can have in a community are silence and fear. The greatest enemy is public reaction. In some communities, city officials have made a public statement of opposition to hate groups. Citizens have carried anti-Klan signs and banners or boycotted Klan events altogether. Any of these responses might be enough to discourage Klan recruiting, although protesting at marches increases the potential for violence.

Some communities have gone even farther. A 1987 Klan march in Greensboro, North Carolina, drew 125 people. The day before, about six times as many city officials, ministers of different faiths, police officials, and concerned citizens had gathered for a celebration of racial harmony. By the time the Klan march came along, it looked small and insignificant by comparison.

Many young people across the country have been holding "rainbow rallies"—celebrations of the "rainbow" of skin colors in America—on or near the dates of racist marches. When a rally is held on the same day as a march, it is held in a different part of town.

In 1989, a racist "Skinhead Weekend" was held near Coeur d'Alene, Idaho, to recruit new members to the Aryan Nations, a coalition of white supremacist groups. In response, a group of students and adults organized a "Walk for Racial Equality." An African American man in a wheelchair led the walk, followed by more than 1,000 people from all over the Northwest.

Walking for racial equality in Coeur d'Alene, Idaho

CHRIS ANDERSON, SPOKANE SPOKESMAN-REVIEW

A major Ku Klux Klan rally is held one weekend each year in Pulaski, Tennessee, considered by members to be the birthplace of the Klan. In 1989, Klan members marched in a nearly empty town because businesses had closed for the weekend and hung orange banners symbolizing harmony. In 1990, citizens of all ages organized a "Brotherhood" march for the same weekend.

In 1990 in Reno, Nevada, a group called Teenagers Against Racial Prejudice held its first Human Rights Day with help from the National Conference. Events included a candlelight vigil for a black man killed by two racists.

If you hear that the Klan or another hate group is coming to your town, you might want to try one of these strategies:

- Work with community leaders to organize a protest. Choose protesters who won't be drawn into name-calling, harassment, and fights with Klan members or skins. It's important to make a commitment to stage a *peaceful* protest.

- Schedule free entertainment in another part of town. This will help to attract the curious away from the racist events.

- To build community solidarity before an incident, try some "fence mending." Ordinarily, the phrase "to mend fences" means "to make peace." In this case, take it literally, too. Organize a neighborhood fix-up day or weekend. Paint front doors, trim fences, rake leaves, mend fences, and get to know your neighbors better in the process. The Miami Police Department does this every year in the Little Haiti Community. In such a large, impersonal city, it's one way they can form better relationships with the people they serve.

Portions of this section were adapted from "Saying No to the Klan" in *The Ku Klux Klan: A History of Racism and Violence* (1991) by Klanwatch, a project of the Southern Poverty Law Center. Used with permission.

1.　Why do you think Hitler ordered gypsies and Jehovah's Witnesses killed as well as Jews?

2.　The White Student Union, a college organization believed to be racist by many watchdog groups, argues in defense of their organization: "If African American students, women, and gays and lesbians have their own groups, why shouldn't white students get together to celebrate their heritage?" How would you respond?

3.　Overheard at a library: A boy about eight years old asks his father, "How come there's no white history month?" How would you answer?

4.　Where do you think skinheads learn that violence is an appropriate way to express anger and resolve conflict?

5.　How did you learn to deal with anger and conflict? Do you feel that you deal with them in positive and effective ways?

Getting along in a changing world...

CityKids: By Kids, For Kids, About Kids

"Yeah, we all know racism exists.
But we also have to take some of the responsibility."

Former gang leader

A Chinese American teenager suffers silently when neighbors make fun of her "slanty eyes." An Asian boy gets called an "illegal alien" by his classmates and pretends he doesn't hear. An overweight girl bitterly endures taunts about her size, too insecure to stand up for herself.

At least, that's how things are at the beginning of a rap video called "What'Cha Gonna Do About Hate?" produced by CityKids, a multicultural organization composed of young people ages 13 to 22 who are devoted to teaching kids how to confront the issues that affect their lives.

Through live performances in New York and Los Angeles schools, television programs, anti-bias conferences, mural painting projects, and public testimonies from members who credit the group with turning their lives around, CityKids models positive values like self-esteem and self-respect.

NATHAN ENGLANDER, 1993

Young people during a scene from a CityKids video

Everything they do is inspired by real-life experiences of young people. People like 17-year-old Kenneth, a former skinhead, and James, a former gang leader whose face is still scarred from the time a rival broke a bottle against his face.

James, now a CityKids member, told a group of 150 people at a community forum in Harlem: "Yeah, we all know racism exists, that it's still a white world. But we also have to take some of the responsibility and blame: kids not respecting each other or Mrs. Jones down the block. Kids killing each other."

The "What'Cha Gonna Do About Hate?" video features a group of CityKids transforming a wall covered with hate graffiti into a "Wall of Love." The kids featured at the beginning of the video go through some changes, too. The Chinese girl confronts the creeps who have been hassling her, they back down, and her little sister beams with pride. The next time somebody calls the

Asian boy an "illegal alien," he shoots back, "Do I look like E.T. to you?" And the overweight girl? She boasts, "I think I'm so good God made more of me."

To find out more about CityKids, write or call:

The CityKids Foundation
57 Leonard Street
New York, NY 10013
Telephone: (212) 925-3320

Resources

Books

The Amish School by Sara E. Fisher and Rachael K. Stahl (Intercourse, PA: Good Books, 1986).

Becoming Myself: True Stories about Learning from Life by Cassandra Walker Simmons (Minneapolis: Free Spirit Publishing Inc., 1994).

Bridges of Respect: Creating Support for Gay & Lesbian Youth (Philadelphia: American Friends Service Committee, 1989).

Chinatown: A Portrait of a Closed Society by Gwen Kinkead (New York: HarperCollins, 1992).

City Safaris: A Sierra Club Explorer's Guide to Urban Adventures for Grownups and Kids by Carolyn Shaffer and Erica Fielder (San Francisco: Sierra Books, 1987).

The Coping With Series (New York: The Rosen Publishing Group):
- *Coping With a Bigoted Parent* by Maryann Miller (1992)
- *Coping With Discrimination* by Gabrielle Edwards (1992)
- *Coping in an Interfaith Family* by Gwen Packard (1993)
- *Coping With Interracial Dating* by Renea Nash (1993)

An Exceptional View of Life, written and illustrated by children with disabilities (CA: A Child's Point of View Special Publication, 1977).

Eyes on the Prize: America's Civil Rights Years, 1954–1965 by Juan Williams (New York: Penguin Books, 1987).

Hands around the World: 365 Ways to Build Cultural Awareness and Global Respect by Susan Milord (Charlotte, VT: Williamson Publishing, 1992).

I, Rigoberta Menchu: An Indian Woman in Guatemala by Rigoberta Menchu (New York: Verso, 1984).

Move Over, Wheelchairs Coming Through! Seven Young People in Wheelchairs Talk about Their Lives by Ron Roy (New York: Clarion Books, 1985).

My Soul Is Rested: The Story of the Civil Rights Movement in the Deep South by Howell Raines (New York: Penguin Books, 1983).

Nobody Nowhere: The Extraordinary Autobiography of an Autistic by Donna Williams (New York: Times Books, 1992).

Plain and Simple: A Woman's Journey to the Amish by Sue Bender (New York: HarperCollins, 1989).

Rising Voices: Writings of Young Native Americans (Riverside, NJ: MacMillan Publishing Co., 1992).

Straight Talk about Prejudice by Rachel Kranz (New York: Facts on File, Inc., 1992).

Understanding Arabs: A Guide for Westerners by Margaret K. Nydell (Yarmouth, ME: Intercultural Press Inc., 1989).

United They Hate: White Supremacist Groups in America by Michael Kronenwetter (New York: Walker and Company, 1992).

The Values Library (New York: The Rosen Publishing Group)

- *Compassion* by Alice Margulies (1990)
- *Cooperation* by Sherry Marker (1991)
- *Tolerance* by Kevin Osborn (1993)

When Someone You Know Is Gay by Susan and Daniel Cohen (New York: M. Evans & Company, 1989).

Wisdomkeepers: Meeting with Native American Spiritual Elders (Hillsboro, OR: Beyond Words Publishing, 1993).

Music

Township jive, salsa, zydeco, klezmer, zouk—there's a lot more to music than rock, rap, jazz, blues, and country. And people from different cultures and musical traditions are blending their styles and ideas and making music that's unlike anything that went before. For instance, a Native American/African American rap group called Boyz from the Rez is working on a rock opera about the life of the great chief, Sitting Bull.

Since music is communication about culture, listening is a wonderful way to explore new territory. As musicians around the globe continue to influence one another, the result is imaginative, exciting blends of sound that challenge our capacity to categorize them.

So you may hear phrases like "ambient-kinetic soundscape," "techno-tribal fusion," and "progressive ethno-pop." But don't be confused or intimidated by the labels, because you may like the music. Here are a few suggestions to get you acquainted with world music, sometimes called "world beat."

"Dancing with the Enemy" and "Rei Momo" (David Byrne/Luaka Bop–Sire)

Cuban top-ten radio hits and South American-inspired dance music, these recordings are part of Byrne's 17-year musical experiment that began with the alternative rock group Talking Heads. Innovative and unpredictable, this Scottish musician has produced recordings of South American music, scored alternative operas and avant-garde dance performances, and written the music for *True Stories*, a movie about the eccentric residents of tiny Virgil, Texas, co-written with Mississippi playwright Beth Henley. Also, with Brian Eno, progressive electronic art rock guru, Byrne has recorded "My Life in the Bush of Ghosts" (Warner), which combines to spooky, hypnotic effect the rantings of radio evangelists, tribal vocalizations, and African drums. Byrne's recordings have been described as "Third World funk," "brain music and dance music," and "stylistically all over the map," with "witty oddball lyrics."

"Deep Forest" (Celine Music)

A blending of forest sounds and the traditional chants of African tribal groups, including pygmies.

"Global Celebration" (Ellipses Arts)

This four-CD, four-cassette set is a musical education all by itself. It includes Latvian pagan midsummer celebration tunes, Moroccan Rose Harvest festival music, Antilles Creole Festival sounds, and much, much more. Global Celebration has been described as "more than an exercise in exotic tastes…four hours of some of the most stirring music you'll ever hear."

"Graceland" (Paul Simon/Warner)

One of the first mainstream American musicians to introduce multicultural music to a broad audience, Paul Simon presents township jive (South African street music), the South African *a cappella* church singing of Ladysmith Black Mambazo, and zydeco, the Cajun-inspired black dance music of southwest Louisiana. On "Graceland," Simon also works with Los Lobos, a popular Latino group from East Los Angeles, and zydeco group Good Rockin' Dopsie and The Twisters. Always an experimenter, Simon's pop music also has been influenced by Brazilian music, reggae, and rhythm and blues. (Note: Cajun groups usually consist of a fiddle, accordion, and guitar player. They perform energetic dance tunes, nicknamed "chank-a-chank" because that's how the repetitious rhythm sounds, and sentimental love songs—all in Cajun French, a language of Louisiana's bayou country.)

"Irish Heartbeat" (Van Morrison & The Chieftains/Mercury)

The Chieftains are one of the longest-lived, best-known Irish musical groups in the world. (Another is the more contemporary group Clannad.) Van Morrison, an Irish vocalist with an equally successful solo career, joins the group in heartbreaking, melancholy ballads and giddy jigs and reels.

"La Mystere des Voix Bulgares" (Nonesuch, volumes 1 and 2, and Fontana, volume 3)

"The Mysterious Voices of Bulgaria" is a 23-member women's choir that performs richly varied folk songs in piercing, ethereal harmonies. The recordings feature songs from various regions of Bulgaria including whooping solos and duets, mournful chorales and brisk work songs. Instrumental accompaniment is performed on traditional instruments: a long, wooden flute played lengthwise like a recorder; a long-necked mandolin; a small violin; and bagpipes.

"Nouveau Flamenco" (Ottmar Liebert/Higher Octave Music)

A classically trained acoustic guitarist born in Germany to a German-American father and a Hungarian mother, Liebert lives in Santa Fe, New Mexico. He borrows traditional Spanish flamenco rhythms (used to accompany flamenco dancers) but gives his music a "nouveau" (new) flavor by adding synthesizers to emulate the sounds of water and voices, and also by playing a Japanese koto (13 strings stretched over an oblong box), two types of flamenco guitars, and a fretless lute. "Nouveau Flamenco" features magical, sparkling melodies described as "acoustic poetry with elegance and passion."

"100% Fortified Zydeco" (Buckwheat Zydeco/Blacktop)

A combination of high-spirited, foot-stompin' Cajun dance music with black rhythm and blues. Using traditional zydeco instruments—accordion, electric bass, horns, keyboards, and a metal rubboard, worn on the chest and stroked with thimbles—Buckwheat Zydeco plays a modernized version of this unique music that was first recorded in 1928 and was played and sung for generations only in the Louisiana bayous.

"A Passage in Time" (Dead Can Dance/Ryko)

Dead Can Dance is an Australian group that uses Gregorian chant (ancient music sung without accompaniment in the early Roman Catholic church) and Celtic music to create a soaring, haunting modern-medieval sound. Their instruments include a Chinese hammered dulcimer and a European hurdy-gurdy, an instrument played by turning a crank.

"Planet Drum" (Mickey Hart/Rounder)

Mickey Hart, drummer for The Grateful Dead, has spent years exploring the role of drumming and music and other cultures. Several solo recordings (and others featuring Dead members) reflect his continuing fascination; his "DIGA" (Rounder Records) was one of the earliest attempts at non-Western inspired recording, now called "world beat" or "world music." Hart also wrote and performed much of the soundtrack for the film *Apocalypse Now,* released as "The Apocalypse Now Sessions" (Rounder). His popular, groundbreaking all-percussion "Planet Drum" followed a group of recordings made during his extensive world travels and "Music to be Born By," inspired by the heartbeat of his son before birth.

"Sundance Season" (R. Carlos Nakai/Celestial Harmonies)

A musician and anthropologist with Navajo-Ute ancestry, Nakai plays his own meditative compositions on a traditional Native American cedar flute sometimes accompanied by chanting, nature sounds, and Tibetan bells. "Sundance Season" was recorded in an open-air cathedral in Colorado.

* * *

You can find out about similar recordings by paging through music catalogs. You might want to start with these:

- The Echo Disk Catalog; call (215) 458-1100.
- The Bose Express; call toll-free 1-800-451-BOSE (451-2673). The cost of the catalog will be applied to your first purchase.
- Rykodisk, Pickering Wharf, Building C-3G, Salem, MA 01980.
- Shanachie Records, P.O. Box 208, Newton, NJ 07860.

Films

Check out these films from the prize-winning PBS series, P.O.V. (a filmmaking term for "Point of View"), dealing with the diversity of modern American life. Some may be available at your local library or neighborhood video store.

P.O.V. is a presentation of KCET/Los Angeles, South Carolina ETV, WGBH/Boston, and WNET/New York. To find out if a film is available on video, write to:

P.O.V. Home Video
c/o New Video Group
419 Park Avenue South, 20th Floor
New York, NY 10016

"Absolutely Positive," Peter Adair, produced by Janet Cole, co-presented by P.O.V. and KQED/San Francisco

Filmmaker Peter Adair asked 11 people—men and women, gay and straight, from all walks of life—to share their stories about having the HIV virus. Alternately irreverent, candid, and moving, this film is not about being sick; it is about being true to the emotional complexity of being human.

"Acting Our Age," Michal Aviad, Direct Cinema, Ltd.

"There's nobody not going to get old—unless they die," says Enola Maxwell at the beginning of this engaging and refreshing film. Through the eyes of six women ages 65–75, we see a variety of perspectives on aging, changing body image, sexuality, family life, and dealing with death.

"American Tongues," Louis Alvarez and Andrew Kolker, Center for New American Media

Rich in humor and regional pride, this hilarious film uses language to reveal our attitudes about other people. From Cajun teenagers to Texas cowboys, "American Tongues" contains funny, provocative, and often telling comments on American diversity.

"Best Boy," Ira Wohl, International Film Exchange

Winner of an Academy Award for Best Feature Documentary, "Best Boy" is the moving story of Philly, a 53-year-old retarded man who adapts to an independent life as he prepares to move away from his elderly parents.

"Color Adjustment," Marlon Riggs, California Newsreel and National Black Programming Consortium

From "Amos 'n' Andy" to "Nat King Cole," from "Roots" to the "Cosby" show, blacks have played many roles on prime time television. "Color Adjustment" blends humor, insight, and thoughtful analysis to explore the evolution of black/white relations as reflected by America's favorite pastime.

"Days of Waiting," Steven Okazaki, Mouchette Films

Artist Estelle Peck Ishigo went with her Japanese American husband into an internment camp during World War II, one of the few Caucasians to do so. Vividly recreated from Ishigo's own memoirs, photos, and paintings, "Days of Waiting" reveals the shattering relocation from an "outsider's" point of view.

"The Family Album," Alan Berliner

Watching "The Family Album" is like coming across a long-lost box of family photos; it's enchanting, funny, and sometimes bizarre. Director Alan Berliner spent years blending home movies and tape recordings collected from 60 American families to assemble a "composite lifetime" which moves from childhood to adulthood, from innocence to experience.

"Fast Food Women," Anne Lewis Johnson, Appalshop, Inc.

Women across the nation are frying chicken, making pizzas, and flipping burgers for fast food chains, struggling to support families in communities hard-hit by a failing economy. "Fast Food Women" documents the jobs of the "working poor."

"Green Streets," Maria De Luca, De Luca Films

If a tree can grow in Brooklyn, can an eggplant survive in the Bronx? "Green Streets" tells the story of the spontaneous growth of community gardens in New York City and how they've helped nourish neighborhood pride, racial tolerance, and a budding sense of hope for hundreds of enthusiastic gardeners in the urban jungles.

"Honorable Nations," Chana Gazit and David Steward, P.O.V.

For 99 years, the residents of Salamanca, New York, have rented the land under their homes for $1 per year from the Seneca Indians, under the terms of a lease imposed by Congress. Now, as the lease is about to expire, a century of bad business must be renegotiated. "Honorable Nations" captures the unfolding drama as the survival of an American town and justice for the Senecas seem to be in conflict.

"Lost Angeles," Tom Seidman, P.O.V.

A powerful, intimate look at the struggles of a group of homeless people who have been moved to an "urban campground" in Los Angeles. Made with the help of a crew that included campground "residents," the film graphically portrays the harsh realities of life on the streets.

"Takeover," Pam Yates and Peter Kinoy, Skylight Productions, funded by Bruce Springsteen

"We're dying in the streets—that should be against the law," say the homeless men and women in this film. It was shot simultaneously in eight U.S. cities on May 1, 1990, as homeless people risked arrest occupying properties foreclosed by the Federal government.

"Who Killed Vincent Chin?," Christine Choy and Renee Tajima, co-produced by WTVS, Detroit

On a hot summer night in Detroit, Ronald Ebens, an unemployed autoworker, killed a young Chinese-American engineer with a baseball bat because of Ebens' resentment for Japanese automakers. Although he confessed, Ebens never spent a day in jail. This Academy Award-nominated film explores the lives of the families involved and the American justice system.

Organizations, Destinations, and Events

Birmingham Civil Rights Institute

Birmingham, AL; (205) 328-9696. Located in the city's Civil Rights District, the Institute offers an overview of the African American struggle for civil rights through films and exhibits, such as a replica of a "whites only" snack bar, separate water fountains, and a segregated bus. The Institute also is a research facility with education programs directed at schools and public audiences.

Black Heritage Trail

Boston, MA; (617) 742-5415 or (617) 742-1854. More than a dozen buildings and monuments are included in a guided or self-guided historical and architectural tour of Boston's African American community, which predates the Civil War.

Camp It Up

1524 McGee Avenue, Berkeley, CA 94703; (510) 530-0107. Not far from Yosemite National Park, families of all kinds swim, go hiking and stargazing, and enjoy arts and crafts classes together. Everyone is welcome: single parent, gay and lesbian, multicultural, and traditional families, with or without children. The camp also provides opportunities for adults to discuss their concerns.

Carnaval Miami

Little Havana, Miami, FL; (305) 644-8888. Music, dance groups, puppet shows, folk dances, parades, concerts, fireworks, and food fill 50 stages and cover 24 blocks at the nation's largest Hispanic celebration. The festivities last for over a week each March.

Chilkat Indian Dancers

Haines, AK; for performance information, call toll-free 1-800-458-3579. These dancers wear colorful tribal masks and demonstrate Tlingit dancing at various times during the year.

Chinese Culture Center

San Francisco, CA; (415) 986-1822. Exhibits, programs, concerts, and classes teach about the culture and traditions of China. The Center also sponsors walking tours of Chinatown.

Christmas at the Palace of Governors on the Plaza

Santa Fe, NM; (505) 827-6483. Several days of music, storytelling, and craft displays; on Christmas Eve, farolitos (sand-filled paper bags with candles inside) line the courtyards and walkways to light the way for the Christ Child.

Cinco de Mayo

Phoenix, AZ; (602) 542-8687; Los Angeles, CA; (213) 625-5045; San Francisco, CA; (415) 826-1401; Portland, OR; (503) 275-9750. Parades, food, dancing, and fun commemorate the Mexican defeat of the French in an important battle for Mexican independence. Phoenix, Los Angeles, San Francisco, and Portland are just four of the many cities that still celebrate the victory on May 5th each year.

Dr. Laz & The CURE

Project CURE, Suite 213, 383 Kingston Avenue, Brooklyn, NY 11213. See pages 67–70 for a profile of this unusual rap group.

Facing History and Ourselves

16 Hurd Road, Brookline, MA 02146; (617) 232-1595. Has developed a Holocaust education program for teachers and provides related resources, including testimonies of survivors of Hitler's death camps.

Ginza Holiday/Bon Odori, Midwest Buddhist Temple

Chicago, IL: (312) 943-7801. Two Asian festivals are celebrated here—the Ginza Holiday (Japanese Cultural Festival in August) and the Bon Odori Festival in July. Cultural displays, dancers wearing kimonos, and other events enlighten visitors about Japanese and Buddhist traditions.

Highlander Research and Education Center

Youth Programs, 1959 Highlander Way, Newmarket, TN 37820; (615) 933-3443. Highlander's two-week residential summer youth workshop brings together 15–20 young people ages 16–19 from culturally diverse backgrounds. Selected by activist community organizations, students explore together their community problems and learn from each other how to be more effective leaders. Graduates may work on intern projects, voter registration drives, transportation projects for senior citizens, and peer tutoring. A famous Highlander graduate: Rosa Parks.

Indian Pueblo Cultural Center

Albuquerque, NM; (505) 843-7270. A market where crafts and art are sold, weekend craft and dance demonstrations are held, and a restaurant serves traditional and native foods. Many pueblos in the area also allow visitors to observe dances and seasonal celebrations.

The Iowa Peace Institute

Box 480, Grinnell, IA 50112; (515) 236-4880. The Institute sponsors a Grinnell Peace Project Award for students in grades 5–12. Individuals and groups are invited to submit completed projects or proposals that promote peace or nonviolent solutions to conflict. Call or write for guidelines.

Mainstrasse Village

Covington, KY; (606) 261-8844 or toll-free 1-800-354-9718. This restored 19th-century German neighborhood of shops and restaurants covers six blocks. Maifest, one of the town's many festivals, is held in mid-May and offers German foods, craft exhibits, and music.

Morikami Museum Park and Gardens

Delray Beach, FL; (407) 495-0233. Three seasonal celebrations honor early Japanese settlers. Ohshogatsu (Japanese New Year) is held in late December to mid-January; the Hatsume Fair celebrates the coming of spring in late February; and the O-Bon Festival in mid-August celebrates summer with dancing, music, and floating paper lanterns.

Museum of Oriental Cultures

Corpus Christi, TX; (512) 883-1303. Dolls, Buddhas, and models of pagodas, shrines, and temples are on display at this museum, along with art from Japan, China, the Philippines, and other Asian countries.

Museum of Tolerance

Los Angeles, CA; (310) 553-8403. Interactive exhibits with recorded racial and sexual slurs force visitors to confront their prejudices. Visitors watch a videotape of Rodney King being beaten and are asked how it affects them. The second half of the museum, which includes a replica of the gates of Auschwitz, deals with the Holocaust. In the Hall of Testimony, the last stop, visitors view videotaped personal accounts of Holocaust survivors.

The NAMES Project

310 Townsend Street, Suite 310, San Francisco, CA 94107; (415) 863-1966. Young people who have had friends, family, or teachers die from AIDS can make a quilt panel in their honor to include in the gigantic 20,000-panel memorial Quilt shown in cities throughout the United States. Begun in 1987, the Quilt is a powerful educational tool, affecting everyone who sees it.

National Museum of American Jewish History

Philadelphia, PA; (215) 923-3811. Special displays focus on the role played by Jews in the growth and development of America from 1954 to the present.

National Youth Leadership Council

1910 West County Road B, St. Paul, MN 55113-1337; (612) 631-3672. Through environmental action groups, international service projects, multicultural projects, and those addressing racism and sexism, NYLC is dedicated to developing leadership and service skills in young people to increase their capacity to benefit their homes, friends, communities, country, and the world.

The People's Place

Intercourse, PA; (717) 768-7171. The film shown at this cultural center promotes a greater understanding and appreciation of the Amish and Mennonite people, who still live an 18th-century, pre-electric existence, plowing with mules and traveling in horsedrawn buggies. Amish World, a hands-on museum, is nearby.

Red Earth Native American Cultural Festival

Oklahoma City, OK; (405) 427-5228. Members of native tribes from the United States and Canada assemble on the first weekend in June for one of the largest Native American gatherings in the world, with several days of traditional competition, dance, music, films, lectures, and a parade.

Totem Poles

Reading from top to bottom, totem poles tell the history of Alaskan and other Northwest native tribes. The animals, monsters, or supernatural creatures carved on the poles may mark a marriage or other special occasion or honor ancestors. If you see a figure carved upside down, you're looking at a "shame pole," carved to ridicule someone. Following are some of the places in Alaska and Washington State where you can see totem poles:

- Fireman's Park, Tacoma, WA, South Ninth and A Streets. A 105-foot cedar totem pole carved by Alaskan Indians is one of the tallest in the U.S.

- Saxman Native Village, two and one-half miles south of Ketchikan, Alaska, on South Tongass Highway.

- Sitka National Historic Park, six miles south of Sitka, Alaska. There's a visitors' center at Metlakatla and Lincoln Streets, one-half mile from town.

- Totem Bight State Historic Site, ten and one-half miles north of Ketchikan, Alaska, on North Tongass Highway.

United States Holocaust Memorial Museum

Washington, DC; (202) 488-0400. The museum has been over-whelmed with visitors since it opened in 1993. When they enter the museum, each visitor is given an identification card and "becomes" a real person who lived during the Holocaust. Only after seeing life-size photographs of Jews killed in a concentration camp, walking through a train car that carried Jews to the death camps, and listening to Nazi propaganda speeches does the visitor learn if the person lived or died.

Much of this section has been excerpted from *Books on the Move: A Read-About-It, Go-There Guide to America's Best Family Destinations* by Susan M. Knorr and Margaret Knorr (Minneapolis: Free Spirit Publishing, 1993). Used with permission of the publisher. Thanks also to *Teaching Tolerance* magazine for several ideas and descriptions.

Bibliography

Books

All Music Guide: The Best CDs, Albums and Tapes edited by Michael Erlewine and Scott Bultman (San Francisco: Miller Freeman, Inc., 1992).

American Indian Stories: Sarah Winnemucca by Mary Frances Morrow (Milwaukee: Raintree Publishers, 1990).

Anti-Bias Curriculum: Tools for Empowering Young Children (Washington, DC: National Association for the Education of Young Children, 1989).

Asian Pacific Americans: A Handbook on How to Cover and Portray Our Nation's Fastest Growing Minority Group by the National Conference of Christians and Jews, Asian American Journalists Associations, and Association of Asian Pacific American Artists (Los Angeles, CA: The National Conference of Christians and Jews, 1989).

Class of 2000: Family Stories—A Teacher's Guide by Betty J. Belanus, Ph.D. (Washington, DC: National Public Radio Special Projects, 1991).

Class of 2000: The Prejudice Puzzle, A Teachers' Guide by Betty J. Belanus, Ph.D. (Washington, DC: National Public Radio Special Projects, 1990).

Cultural Etiquette: A Guide for the Well-Intentioned by Amoja Three Rivers (Indian Valley, VA: Market Wimmin, 1991).

Ellis Island: Echoes from a Nation's Past, A Celebration of the Gateway to

America edited by Susan Jones, editor (New York: Aperture, Inc. in association with the National Park Service, the U.S. Department of the Interior, 1989).

Embracing Diversity: Teacher's Voices from California Classrooms by Laurie Olsen and Nina A. Mullen (San Francisco, CA: California Tomorrow, Immigrant Students Project, 1990).

Esperanto: The World Interlanguage compiled by George Alan Connor, Doris Tappan Connor, William Solzbacher, and the Very Rev. Dr. J.B. Si-Tsien Kao (London: Thomas Yoselhoff, 1966).

Eye to Eye: How People Interact by Peter Marsh (Topsfield, MA: Salem House Publishers, 1988).

Eyes on the Prize: America's Civil Rights Years 1954–1965 by Juan Williams with the Eyes on the Prize Production Team (New York: Penguin Books, 1987).

Fighting Fair: Dr. Martin Luther King, Jr. for Kids by Fran Schmidt and Alice Friedman (Miami Beach, FL: Grace Contrino Abrams Peace Foundation, 1990).

Hate Crime: A Sourcebook for Schools Confronting Bigotry, Harassment, Vandalism, and Violence by Cristina Bodinger-deUriarte with Anthony R. Sancho (Los Alamitos, CA: Southwest Regional Laboratory, undated).

Hate Violence and White Supremacy: A Decade Review 1980–1990 edited by Sara Bullard (Montgomery, AL: Klanwatch, a project of the Southern Poverty Law Center, 1989).

The Ku Klux Klan: A History of Racism and Violence edited by Sara Bullard (Montgomery, AL: Klanwatch, a project of the Southern Poverty Law Center, 1991).

New Voices: Immigrant Students in U.S. Public Schools by Juan McCarty and John Willshire Carrera (Boston, MA: The National Coalition of Advocates for Students, 1991).

Night Riders in Black Folk History by Gladys-Marie Fry (Athens, GA: University of Tennessee Press, 1977).

150 Ways Teens Can Make a Difference: A Handbook for Action by

Marian Salzman and Teresa Reisgies with several thousand teenage contributors (Princeton, NJ: Peterson's Guides, 1991).

Outward Dreams: Black Inventors and Their Inventions by Jim Haskins (New York: Walker and Company, 1991).

Slavery: A World History by Milton Meltzer (New York: De Capo Press, Inc., 1993).

Straight Talk about Prejudice by Rachel Kranz (New York: Facts on File, 1992).

Understanding Arabs: A Guide for Westerners by Margaret K. Nydell (Yarmouth, ME: Intercultural Press, Inc., 1987).

Understanding Physical Anthropology and Archaeology by Robert Jurmain, Harry Nelson, and William A. Turnbaugh (St. Paul, MN: West Publishing Company, 1987).

United They Hate: White Supremacist Groups in America by Michael Kronenwetter (New York: Walker and Company, 1992).

World Beat: A Listener's Guide to Contemporary World Music on CD (Pennington, NJ: A Cappella Books, 1992).

Articles

"A Child of the Movement," *Teaching Tolerance*, Spring 1992, pp. 51-53.

Berger, Joseph, "Immigrants Jam Schools, Invigorating a System," *New York Times*, April 26, 1992, page 6.

Cardinale, Anthony, *Buffalo Magazine* (magazine of *The Buffalo News*), "The Man in the Middle," June 7, 1992.

"Deadly Hate Violence at Record Levels Across the Nation in 1992," *Klanwatch Intelligence Report*, February 1993, pp. 4-5.

Duke, Lynn, "Writing Africa into History," *San Francisco Chronicle (Washington Post)*, March 14, 1993, page 2.

Eaton, Tracey, Weber, Tracy, and Nicolosi, Michelle, "White power's new warriors blend in," *San Francisco Examiner (Orange County Register)*, August 1, 1993, pp. B-1, B-5.

FitzGerald, Nora, "Lily Yeh's Miracle Mosaic," *Applause*, June 1992, pp. 21-22.

"Gay Clout: The New Power Brokers," *Newsweek*, May 3, 1993, page 45.

Greer, Colin, "We Must Take A Stand," *Parade Magazine*, April 28, 1991, pp. 4-6.

Hall, Alice J., "Immigration Today," *National Geographic* magazine, September 1990, pp. 103-105.

Heller, Carolyn, and Williams, Elsie, "Sadako and the Thousand Paper Cranes," *Teaching Tolerance*, Spring 1993, pp. 47-54.

Keeler, Judith, "Dr. Laz and Project CURE," *World of Lubavitch*, April 1993.

Lambert, Lake, "The Movement: The Selma to Montgomery March," *Teaching Tolerance*, Spring 1992, page 56.

Mabry, Marcus (with bureau reports), "Pin a Label on a Manager and Watch What Happens," *Newsweek*, May 14, 1990, page 43.

"Marge's Mouth: The Cincinnati Reds' owner sparks a furor over alleged racial remarks," *Time*, December 7, 1992, page 29.

Meek, Michael, "The Peacekeepers: Students use mediation skills to resolve disputes," *Teaching Tolerance*, Fall 1992, pp. 46-52.

Novogrodsky, Myra, "A Toronto Teacher Reflects on Eight Years with FHAO," *Facing History and Ourselves News*, Winter 1989-90, pp. 8-9.

Robinson, Kathryn, "The Hate Boom," *The Weekly* (Seattle), July 17, 1991, pp. 37-43.

Stein, Judith, "A Village with a Heart," *Metropolitan Home*, July/August 1993, page 35.

Stoskopf, Alan, "Examining Historical Roots to Racism and Antisemitism: A Profile of Facing History's Research," *Facing History and Ourselves News*, Fall 1991, pp. 1, 19-21.

"Talk About It! Democracy Begins in Conversation," *Teaching Tolerance,* Fall 1992, pp. 53-56.

Tilove, Jonathan, "Building Bridges: In divided Memphis, camp brings together black and white teens," *The Birmingham News* (Newhouse News Service), August 2, 1992, page 6-G.

Wise, Michael Z., "Yo! Oy Vey!—Rap It Away," *San Francisco Chronicle (Washington Post),* January 10, 1993.

Videos/Films

"Yeah You Rite!," Louis Alvarez and Andrew Kolker, Center for New American Media, 524 Broadway, 2nd Floor, New York, NY 10012.

"Black History: Lost, Strayed or Stolen," 1991, Xenon Home Video, 211 Arizona Avenue, Santa Monica, CA 90401.

"Seasonal Differences: Constitutional Rights," 1988, produced by Multimedia Entertainment, distributed by Barr Films, P.O. Box 7878, Irwindale, CA 91706-7878.

"Valuing Diversity: New Tools for a New Reality," 1990, Copeland Griggs Productions, 302 23rd Avenue, San Francisco, CA 94121.

Audios

"Class of 2000: Family Stories," 1991, National Public Radio Special Projects, 2025 M Street, Washington, DC 20036.

"Class of 2000: Prejudice Puzzle," 1991, National Public Radio Special Projects, 2025 M Street, Washington, DC 20036.

Index

Index

About the Author

Lynn Duvall has been a writer since she was 13 years old, when she was the first-ever female sports reporter for her middle school newspaper. Since then, she has written for magazines, newspapers, and newsletters about topics including immigration, homelessness, AIDS, popular culture, and the arts. She spent a year as a writer/researcher with Klanwatch, a project of the Southern Poverty Law Center, where she wrote about multicultural issues.

Lynn studied urban anthropology at the University of Alabama at Birmingham and lives nearby in a diverse neighborhood. Her neighbors are Asian Indian, Vietnamese, Palestinian, black, white, Muslim, Hindu, Catholic, atheist, gay, lesbian, albino, and disabled.

MORE FREE SPIRIT BOOKS

The Power to Prevent Suicide: A Guide for Teens Helping Teens
by Dr. Richard E. Nelson and Judith C. Galas
Young people have the power to be suicide preventers, and this book provides up-to-date information on who's at risk, explains the warning signs, offers encouragement to reach out to friends in danger, and tells how to get help. Positive, practical, step-by-step advice that can save lives.
Ages 11 and up.
160 pp.; illus.; s/c; 6" x 9"
ISBN 0-915793-70-9; $11.95

Making the Most of Today: Daily Readings for Young People on Self-Awareness, Creativity, and Self-Esteem
by Pamela Espeland and Rosemary Wallner
Quotes from figures including Eeyore, Mariah Carey, and River Phoenix guide you through a year of positive thinking, problem-solving, and practical lifeskills.
Ages 11 and up.
392 pp.; s/c; 4" x 7"
ISBN 0-915793-33-4; $8.95

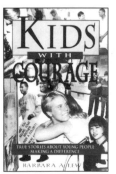

Kids with Courage: True Stories about Young People Making a Difference
by Barbara A. Lewis
Exciting true accounts of kids taking social action, fighting crime, working to save the environment, and performing heroic acts.
Ages 11 and up.
160 pp.; B&W photos; s/c; 6" x 9"
ISBN 0-915793-39-3; $10.95

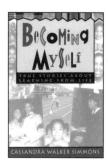

Becoming Myself: True Stories About Learning From Life
by Cassandra Walker Simmons
A TV personality and popular speaker reveals the secrets of her success—self-esteem, strong values, and a supportive family—in dozens of true stories about growing up. Her personal experiences and practical advice will inspire you to believe in yourself and be the winner you are meant to be. Ages 11 and up.
144 pp.; s/c; 5 1/8" x 7 1/2"
ISBN 0-915793-69-5; $4.95

To place an order, or to request a free catalog of
SELF-HELP FOR KIDS® materials, write or call:

Free Spirit Publishing Inc.
400 First Avenue North, Suite 616
Minneapolis, MN 55401-1730
toll-free (800)735-7323, local (612)338-2068